Solutions to Knife crime

A path through the red sea?

Sue Roberts

Series in Sociology

VERNON PRESS

www.vernonpress.com

In the Americas:
Vernon Press
1000 N West Street, Suite 1200
Wilmington, Delaware, 19801
United States

In the rest of the world:
Vernon Press
C/Sancti Espiritu 17,
Malaga, 29006
Spain

Series in Sociology

Library of Congress Control Number: 2020947138

ISBN: 978-1-64889-250-9

Also available: 978-1-62273-942-4 [Hardback]; 978-1-64889-186-1 [PDF, E-Book]

Cover design by Vernon Press

Table of Contents

List of figures and tables

For Callum, Reece, Paul, Dario and Tom.

Thank you

Introduction

This book arose from a two-year project looking into the causes and effects of knife crime in Britain, with special reference to London. The work began in 2018 when the rapid rise in killings and knife offences came to the attention of the public through media reporting. It was with some surprise that I noted, as a former public and civil servant, that the only really hard-hitting and insightful research appeared to be that done by media organisations such as the BBC, ITV, The Guardian, The Independent and others. This surprised me because I expected academics and other experts to be called in to talk about the crisis. However, this was not the case. Many commentators appeared, and powerful testimony from those involved in the violence, and those affected by it, featured strongly in this media research, but there did not seem to be any live academic research featured in the coverage early in 2018.

Later, whilst watching a TV group interview with the mothers of several young people who had died as a result of knife attacks, it became clear that there were significant voices within our communities that may have hitherto gone unnoticed. Over time, I watched many interviews on TV and online with young people who were involved in knife crime, and youth workers who had been trying so hard to make a difference in their communities. I wanted to understand more about where this violence had come from and given my own experience over fifteen years in local and national government, I felt compelled to ask why the voices of young people were not being heard by the central government. Just as important, from my point of view, was the clear role that youth workers, social workers, community development workers, police, community safety and charities could possibly play in making sure the true position was uncovered. Their voices too have not been heard to any great extent and to my knowledge, are not commonly heard and still less acted upon, when they are raised in any public fora. It seems to be the case that civil servants are not routinely included in social research because they are often bound by the Official Secrets Act and both civil and public servants have a strong sense of their ethical responsibilities when working under the terms of their employment in political environments. Speaking out publicly about a major political and societal issue such as knife crime is not within their ambit and carries some risk of sanctions should they do so. However, colleagues and former colleagues were very keen to speak to me about this issue and their words are included in this book. They have a key contribution to make because the public sector provides so many of the support services that the most vulnerable people in society use and it is the case, as we shall see in this book, that knife crime can be associated with the most vulnerable and the most deprived people in our communities.

I began a research project in 2018 looking at the causes of knife crime, using the many contacts I had accumulated arising from my work with local authorities from Merseyside to the south coast, including London, over fifteen years. Here I began speaking to the people involved with young people in every setting; from schools to prisons, from Pupil Referral Units (PRUs) to churches. They were able to put me in touch with the young offenders, gang members and at-risk children who contributed to this research and that of the early study in 2018 (Roberts,2019). I should say that all the young people who kindly participated were unwilling to allow their names or location to appear in the research. In some cases, children and young people asked for their ages to be withheld also. The reasons for this should be obvious. This is an environment in which young people fear for their lives on a daily basis. Any hint as to who may have talked about their activities could result in revenge attacks and these can be, and often are, fatal. The young people know this, and they knew the risk they were taking when they spoke to me. They are also often distrustful of anyone in authority and only tend to put their trust in people who are known to them already or come from their own communities. I have protected their identities at all stages and anonymised contributions from these young people and from individuals from statutory agencies in London and elsewhere.

A handful of contributors have given permission for the transcripts (anonymised) of their interviews to be included in the academic requirements for the publication of evidence under my University. All the public servants I spoke to in my research for this book gave permission for their transcripts to be used by the University of Portsmouth, with the proviso that most wanted to remain anonymous, some out of fear of losing their jobs. Others freely gave permission for their names and locations to be used. I am especially grateful to those of my friends at Police Scotland who were so generously giving of their time and good will. Whilst Glasgow, like London, may sometimes be a violent city, its people welcomed me at every stage in my research and were more than willing to answer my endless questions. It was less easy to gain the complete trust of the children and young people, perhaps because I appeared to some of them at least as a representative of many of the authority figures they so hated. I use this term advisedly because some of the conversations I had were clearly very emotional, with young adults expressing their open hatred of the police and others perceived as associated with them such as probation or prison officers and other authority figures. Mostly, however, these were children and young people who desperately wanted their plight to be heard and understood. The offenders who kindly agreed for me to talk to them were keen to get their point across in terms of the difficulties they faced in their daily lives prior to prison. The irony of this is that some regarded prison as a safe place where they would be fed and sheltered. This struck me as a sad indictment of an increasingly anomic society in which young people feel that their only refuge after a life of extremity on the streets is in a prison.

This book is therefore an attempt to provide a robust, academic investigation into the issue of knife crime, and an attempt to find solutions. It should be said, however, that my paper, published in 2019 about the London Killings (Roberts, 2019) looked at many of the causes. It was with some surprise that virtually all the young people I interviewed, plus the youth and community workers, offered their opinion on what the solutions to knife crime should be. This is the focus of the current research: solutions. We know, or should know by now, that knife crime is a symptom of a society at odds with its most vulnerable people. It is one in which children and young people feel abandoned by the State and this reason alone is why the concept of Anomie fits so well with the theoretical framework. There is a strong feeling among young people that society, politicians, those in positions of power, the police and anyone associated with them have let them down.

In this connection, I cannot say that I interviewed a single child or young adult who was not intelligent, able and articulate. I saw a great deal of untapped potential and neglected talent among these people. I also witnessed the pain and frustration felt by social workers, some distraught and in despair at having to give up roles in their own communities as a result of cuts to public sector spending. Many had lost their jobs, precipitating the loss of decades of experience among some of the most vital community workers and projects. I listened to charity workers who had lost their funding from local government, striving to keep pace with exponential demand from young people who needed support and refuge. I heard from probation officers made redundant through the semi-privatisation of the service who were despairing at having to let down those who depended on them by having to leave the service. It would be no exaggeration to use words such as heartbroken. The public sector was and is peopled with those who care very deeply about their work. Their voices are all included in this book alongside a stricken police service trying to make up the loss of 20,000 officers over the last ten years and contend with the need to save many millions from their budget.

A few years ago, two years after the financial crisis of 2008, I worked in a very deprived community with the children and young people who attended primary and secondary schools in the area. It was with real distress that after a year of continuous work with these children and their parents, I had to tell them the funding for my post had been cut due to the budget reductions in local authority funding by the central government. All the trust that had been painstakingly built over a year was gone the instant I opened my mouth and told them I had to leave. I became just another "bloody official" who had let them down. My story is not unusual and is reflected across the public sector in multiple communities who have lost their support workers. It shows in the interviews undertaken for this book where those who participated have expressed resentment over the loss of their community workers and removal of the very people they relied upon to help them the most.

And yet in spite of all this, the main message of this book is that all is not lost. The remedies for knife crime are there if we can see clearly enough into the causes and then provide the resources and education to take up and apply the right solutions once more. More than anything else, the young people themselves need to know that they are not abandoned, that we can restore their youth clubs, their evening and Saturday football clubs run by community safety staff at the local authority, their community centres, detached youth workers, social workers, community development workers and all the support services around education such as Education Maintenance Allowance (EMA) and housing benefits for young people. It is the loss of these and the absence of community and neighbourhood policing that have contributed so much to the rise in knife crime. As one respondent put it

> "If you take away their places to go, their sanctions for bad behaviour, their support when they get into trouble, their advisory services, their social workers and their neighbourhood police officer, why are we so surprised that they behave like this? The underlying message is – do what you like. We don't care." (R:8. 20 June, 2018)

Ultimately, solutions lie in the restoration of these services: the visibly material redress for all that they feel has been lost. Solutions are put forward by the children and young people themselves in this book, and by those who have worked with them for so long. There are policy changes that we can make and the approach we can take is set out in this book in the section headed "The Case for Policy Transfer." There are lessons we can learn from those who have direct experience of working together to solve violence in communities; the work done and the real achievements made by Cure Violence in the USA and the Violence Reduction Unit in Glasgow are both discussed here. There are workable, tried and tested remedies for our knife crime epidemic in Britain, but they must be led and supported by Government.

As explained, I have included in the research the voices of some of the staff formerly employed by local authorities. It is often the case that the public at large are not fully aware of the range of support services provided by local government, and more importantly, are unaware of the extent of the cuts made to councils at all levels. Additionally, some may not know that local councils have a duty to safeguard vulnerable children and young people under a statutory obligation placed upon them by the Government (House of Lords Library, parliament UK, 2019). It is only now, after the public sector spending cuts, that we are seeing the huge rise in knife offences and homicides when services have been withdrawn by local councils as a result of reductions in funding. Remembering that public sector spending cuts have not excluded other services, Metropolitan Police Commissioner, Cressida Dick made the connection between the loss of funding for policing, the reduction in police numbers and the rise in knife offences when she was quoted as saying

> "……..of course I would be naive to say that the reduction in police finances over the last few years, not just in London but beyond, hasn't had an impact,"[on the rise in knife crime] (Parliament TV, 5 June 2018; Huffington Post, 19 May 2018)

Public sector spending cuts have been a significant contributor to the increase in knife crime. This is why an important section of the book deals with the loss of public services, to which I have added evidential data provided by former local authority personnel to ensure that their voices are not lost in the debate.

A further purpose for this book is to ensure that both primary and secondary research into the problem of knife crime in Britain are presented as part of the academic discourse. I have chosen hermeneutic phenomenology as an element of the theoretical framework for this study because of its emphasis on the significance of context. Without understanding the context in which knife crime proliferates, it will be hard to address the required remedies in any positive and effective way. Context yields the full extent of the issue, laying it bare not just in terms of its causes but also, fully, in terms of the solutions that are necessary. We should therefore begin to look beyond the knife towards the context; to the effects of the public spending cuts and the endemic inequality that exists in British society and gives rise to the persistent deprivation, poverty and prejudices that make the context surrounding the knife so significant. That is what we will do here. In simple terms, things happen for a reason, and reasons accurately understood and then expertly and comprehensively acted upon, can help to provide the solutions.

Note: Where quotes are included from respondents to the interviews for the research in this book, they are referred to by the letter 'R', then the number of the respondent, followed by the date on which the interview took place. For example, (R:1. 19 July, 2019). There are 29 respondents who were recruited through colleagues and contacts in public services in line with the author's experience in the sector. The age range for the young people who participated is from age 9 to age 28. The interview questions followed the same semi-structured pattern used in the author's 2018 paper on the London stabbings of 2018 (Roberts, 2019) and were trialled with professionals before the research began. Where direct permission has not been given for names to be included in this book, respondents have been anonymised.

Chapter 1

The problem with knife crime

This book will not give you a single, silver bullet solution to knife crime-because there is no single solution.

However, there are many possible solutions that must be considered in the light of growing knife crime offences, and we will explore how they work, why they work and where they work best together.

The research is based on two hypotheses:

1. That there are partnership-based policy solutions to knife crime (H1)

2. That the people involved in knife crime can help us to identify solutions to tackle it (H2)

The reason for H1 is derived from the author's experience in government at national and local levels and the leadership and management of multi-agency partnerships. H2 is based on the evidence from the research begun in 2018 in which respondents have suggested solutions for knife crime. It is hoped that the research undertaken for this study will demonstrate, through primary and secondary research, that partnership-based policy solutions to knife crime can indeed be enacted in Britain and that those involved in the violence across all sectors can help to show us the most effective remedies.

The primary research for this book has been done in the UK and the USA through interviews and discussions with a range of people. These include victims and perpetrators, youth workers, social workers, police, police staff, local authority workers, academics, gang members and former gang members, charity leaders and workers and prison officers. The purpose of selecting such a wide group of people is to reflect the second hypothesis: that those with direct involvement can help identify solutions to tackle knife crime effectively, not just on the street but throughout all levels of society. Indeed, the purpose of the book is to help frame credible and workable solutions to knife crime in Britain. It is a crime wave that has frightened and shocked us as young people continue to die in overwhelming numbers. Much attention has been focused on the reasons for such a harrowing crime, but it is essential that as a society we must now turn both our attention and our resources towards solutions.

Chapter 2

Summary of the findings

The key findings from the research are set out below, with recommendations from those who took part.

It must be stated that the findings demonstrate the need for a new direction in tackling knife crime. As stated, there is no single solution to the problem. Instead there are configurations for solutions and circumstances in which a variety of solutions seem to work well. The findings from the research can therefore be distilled into five significant points as follows:

1. **Re-establish links with communities**. It is clear from the loss of police personnel in England and the cuts to public services (Roberts, 2019) that links with communities appear to be badly fractured, and in many cases, broken. Police Community Support Officers (PCSOs) are crucial to this connectedness (Loveday and Smith, 2015; Roberts, 2019) providing vital relationship links to local communities and in some areas of Britain (BBC News, 4 June 2019; Loveday and Smith, 2015), these have been cut. Although attached to police forces, PCSOs establish strong links with communities, enabling them to identify local trouble spots, flashpoints and perpetrators. So too do local authority community safety and community development staff. These vital people are the conduits that lead us to a deeper level of local intelligence in neighbourhoods. Links with communities must be re-established through a variety of people and agencies; Police, PCSOs, community partnerships, community workers and leaders, youth workers, third sector workers, health professionals, local authorities and others.

2. **Deploy people who are part of the community** to liaise with local perpetrators, victims and families to intervene early and help prevent violence. Part of the response, alongside re-establishing links with communities, must be to use those who know the environment and are part of it.

    "It's the lived experience of knife crime that matters here, especially in communities. There's no substitute for it and

no credibility without it when you're looking for
solutions" (R:18. 4 September, 2019)

Similarly, research by this author emphasised the need for community
links (Roberts, 2019) and familiarity with the local area to be able to
tackle the violence.

"It has to be people that have grown up around here and
know the people in the area. Strangers dropping in won't
cut it. It's an issue of trust. Without that you haven't got a
hope." (R:1. 13 July 2019).

It is clear that community credibility is crucial.

3. **Redefine partnership working**. Establish strong local networks as
    well as partnerships that can liaise with each other on a daily basis.
    Violence on this scale requires not just the quarterly meeting of
    statutory agencies in a predetermined venue, but regular, sometimes
    daily interaction between members of local networks. Police in
    Glasgow have made this work and demonstrate strong, effective and
    trusting local networks that interact to help reduce community
    violence. These are explored in this book. It is members of
    communities who need to participate in establishing local networks
    and be prepared to lead. We still need regular meetings of statutory
    agencies, but these can no longer set the agenda in isolation. The lead
    must equally come from local people and local networks.

4. **Reduce the punitive nature of intervention**. McNeill and Wheller's
    2019 briefing paper for the College of Policing affirms that "knife crime
    and weapon carrying cannot be solved by criminal justice measures
    alone" (p.2), adding that "the best approaches are multi-faceted, also
    involving early intervention and multi-agency collaborative working."
    Whilst the measures taken by the police for addressing knife crime
    may be necessary, these cannot constitute the totality of a response to
    knife crime in England. The response must be multi-level, multi-
    agency and multi-faceted, focusing not merely on punishment but on
    a more holistic and human approach. Perry, (R:1. 13 July, 2019) argued
    that we must use different tactics and "stop punishing them over and
    over."

5. **Offer young people real opportunities**. Previous research by the
    author and comments from respondents for the current research
    confirm that the lack of public services, access to educational
    opportunities and training programmes are a problem and a barrier

to systemic change. Young people feel they have no hope for the future (Roberts, 2019), particularly young black people in London and elsewhere.

> "You know, like, what's the point man? None of us, we
> don't got no hope" (R5. 15 July, 2019).

6. **Use the lessons learned from others.** In a section at the end of this book entitled "The Case for Policy Transfer" an exploration of the Scottish knife crime policy demonstrates the cohesion and partnership working that has made their approach to tackling knife crime so successful. Learning lessons from those that are able to reduce knife crime is a common-sense response to the violence. In Britain the government have emulated the model of the Scottish Violence Reduction Unit but have not looked at the wider policy behind it or the connected services that work with the VRU. In "The Case for Policy Transfer" later in this book, an examination of the British and Scottish policy approaches is set out, with recommendations for the future.

But it is not a wholly gloomy picture. There are those who have managed to find a way out of the knife crime cycle. The author visited the Scottish VRUs Street and Arrow project, meeting with a young former offender and perpetrator, himself the victim of multiple stabbing incidents. He has now changed his life through the intervention of the VRU and said:

> "My daughter will never see her dad involved with knives. I've been
> working here for a year; I'm clean from drugs and alcohol, I work and my
> son and my daughter will not have the life I had. They'll see a way out"
> (R: 18. 4 September, 2019)

Chapter 3

Knife crime in Britain

It is a truism that knife crime is now a serious national youth issue in Britain. Young people are killing each other in some areas of the country at a higher rate since records began (The Guardian, 17 October 2019 (e); Parliament UK, October 2020). The graph shown below demonstrates the upward curve in recorded offences from the House of Commons library in Britain. Please note that this graph has excluded the Greater Manchester area.

Figure 3.1 Knife Crime Highest Recorded Level in 9 Years

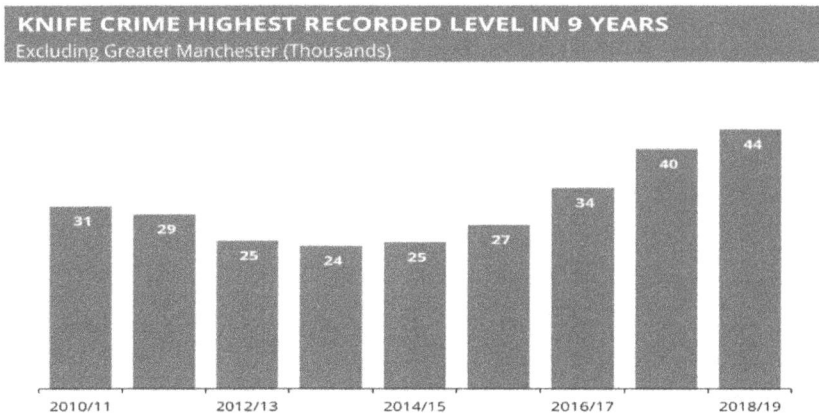

KNIFE CRIME HIGHEST RECORDED LEVEL IN 9 YEARS
Excluding Greater Manchester (Thousands)

(Source: HM Government: House of Commons Library, 20 December 2019).

The debate over knife crime has been the subject of detailed attention both in the media and the academic world, tracking the process of the killings and documenting the reasons for them. Yet with the rate steadily increasing, attention must now be directed towards remedies for knife crime, and it is important to emphasise the plural here. As stated, there is no single solution offered here for knife crime in the UK, as the research will demonstrate. Instead it is recommended that a range of solutions should be enacted simultaneously to address this national scourge (Roberts, 2019; Massey, Sherman and Coupe, 2019; Grimshaw and Ford, 2018). Solutions are explored in this book by those who have been involved including victims, perpetrators, police and a wide range of agencies responding to the crisis, both in the UK and further afield.

They are discussed alongside political, policy-based remedies, reviewing areas where this has been successful, with special reference to Scotland, Chicago and New York. As far as lived experience is concerned, those involved in the research set out evidence which suggests the way forward for knife crime solutions in Britain. It is this personal, lived experience that gives such suggested solutions value and reality in a social climate of suspicion and fear around knife crime. We should therefore spare some time to consider the notion of lived experience from the viewpoint of robustness in social research.

Chapter 4

Lived Experience

The notion of lived experience derives from social psychology and qualitative phenomenological research. It fits very strongly with the concept of hermeneutic phenomenology, (Van Manen, 2016, p. ix) which is part of the theoretical framework for this book and is explained in the following section. Lived experience, in its most immediate form, is defined as something which has phenomenological immediacy and meaning for the individual: something that belongs to that person alone because they have awareness of it. The experience has not been handed to the person in a second-hand way or reported to them by a third party. It is direct.

> "A lived experience does not confront me as something perceived or represented; it is not given to me, but the reality of lived experience is there-for-me because I have a reflexive awareness of it, because I possess it immediately as belonging to me in some sense." (Dilthey in Van Manen, 2016. p. 18)

A lived experience becomes something that can be interpreted through the individual's ability to reflect upon it and make some sense of it after the event. This is especially relevant to us as we explore the lived experience of respondents in this book. The immediacy of a knife attack, either as a victim or witness, or as a professional trying to mitigate the effects, is profoundly disturbing and is an experience requiring deep personal interpretation and reflection. Unsurprisingly, some do not recover well and fall victim to Post Traumatic Stress Disorder (PTSD). Knife crime can often become a traumatic and post-traumatic experience as the individual struggles to come to terms with it. A knife attack is an up-close-and-personal crime, involving victim and perpetrator in very close physical proximity. One of the respondents for the current research, here referred to as respondent 18 (R:18) describes his horrific experience of a knife attack.

> "My story is that I was stabbed nine times on my front door-step. My son saw it all. He was terrified: terrified of me because of it." (4 September, 2019)

This incident took place outside the home, within the neighbourhood and in front of the child of this young man. It was the culmination of many previous experiences with knives and youth violence in Glasgow, but one that put an end to his involvement, not only because of the seriousness of his injuries but because of the psychological effect of his experiences and the effect on his son. The trauma experienced by him and by his little boy reverberated throughout both their lives and the lives of their family and friends, remaining with them to this day. Similarly, when the author interviewed R: 1 (13 July, 2019), he described a life on Staten Island USA as "trauma on top of trauma on top of trauma" for himself as a young man growing up in the area and for the many young people still experiencing youth violence. Although the weapon-type is different in the USA: the preferred weapons are guns rather than knives, the trauma described and the effects of it within the community are without a doubt similar as we will discover in this book. R:1 talked of his early life in which he would walk to school past the place where his father was murdered.

> "I saw my dad murdered in front of me. Every day I passed his blood on the way to school. No one like cleaned it up or nothing. You can see what that was like. Then later on my mom being abused and hurt by men in our house..... I been in jail and stuff. I had those experiences."

Subsequent related traumas coloured his childhood, and as with R: 18 above, both describe early life as a deeply difficult and desperate time for them and for their peers. Both young men came from a background in which extreme deprivation and difficulty characterised their early childhood experiences. The societal context in which these experiences are common bear strong similarities in terms of the adverse childhood experiences (ACES) of victims and perpetrators, the poverty, deprivation, lack of educational chances, lack of opportunity, parental neglect, poor housing and a host of other attendant problems. These are all discussed within this book because they key directly into the notion of context around the individual and connect with General Strain Theory (Agnew, 1992), Anomie and hermeneutic phenomenology. The context is also discussed in terms of the cuts to local authorities in Britain because it is through local authorities that many of the services on which vulnerable people and families depend are provided. The context around knife crime is dealt with at local level, and here councils are at their most active. Therefore, the contention here is that we must begin to look beyond the knife and consider the context in which these youngsters grew up.

Knife crime is a phenomenon that we seem to have discussed endlessly in terms of causes and outcomes, but we must now begin to consider this in terms of what can be done to resolve this phenomenon. Therefore, phenomenology is the framework in which we will discuss possible solutions. We begin this discussion by considering the importance of Lived Experience and its relevance to phenomenology. Van Manen (2016) argues that Lived Experience can be seen as the beginning and the end-point of phenomenology (p.36) and this is the reason why, specifically, hermeneutic phenomenology has been selected as part of the theoretical framework for this book. Through the lived experience of those who have participated in the research, and the lessons we can learn from other policies to address youth violence, it is hoped that we will be able to determine some routes forward in addressing the phenomenon of rising knife crime in Britain. We will also consider the role of partnership and collaborative working in tackling the violence. Statutory agencies, charities and communities can all work together, and have been working together to address knife crime. We must now review the current landscape for partnership working in Britain in line with the recommendations in the Government's Serious Violence Strategy, published in 2018 (HM. Government, 2018).

Chapter 5

Working together

To date, the pressing need for urgent, remedial action for knife crime in England has resulted in the adoption of the Scottish Violence Reduction Unit's (VRU) public health strategy by London Mayor, Sadiq Khan in 2018 (Roberts, 2019; HM Government, 2019 (d)). This approach has proved very successful in Glasgow in combating serious violence and we will examine it in this book. However, it must be strongly emphasised that the Scottish VRU is part of a well-networked, well-supported range of partners working together, as described later in the chapter entitled "The Case for Policy Transfer." The author spent time with Police Scotland as part of the research, working through the various levels of support and resources available to the SVRU. The whole approach is predicated upon collaborative working: agencies and individuals tackling violence together as partners (SVRU, 2020). The value of such an approach should not be underestimated. If the way to address and reduce knife crime is truly to be through working together collaboratively, then we must take the strategy of the Scottish VRU far more seriously. Indeed, the VRU alone is not solely responsible for the reduction in knife crime violence, because the partnerships and networks that support it share joint responsibility with it. Their shared focus is to reduce community violence together, and this includes knife crime. The Scottish policy and its partnership approach is explored in this book in the context of a serious attempt to reduce knife crime and tackle community violence in the round, whatever the source. This aligns to the first hypothesis: that there are partnership-based policy solutions to knife crime.

Chapter 6

Remedial actions

If we consider the idea of establishing VRU's across the country in England, it will become clear that well publicised, single initiatives such as setting up "VRUs" will never be sufficient to address such a complex and embedded problem as we currently face with our young people. Adopting a fragmented approach through distributing money across the country for local areas to set up their own VRUs (Gov.uk, 2020 (b)) without the properly funded, partnership infrastructure that makes the Scottish and the USAs Cure Violence initiatives so successful, does not constitute a recipe for success in Britain.

There is some recognition that the VRU ethos includes partnership working, yet much of the funding in England and Wales for partnership or collaborative working with support and leadership through local authorities has been lost over the last ten years. This will be discussed here. The reduction in local multi-agency partnership working has taken place under the Conservative-led Austerity programme from 2010 -2020 (Roberts, 2016; Roberts, 2019; JRF, 2015 (a); Institute for Government, 2019). Government backing for the supporting collaborative infrastructure which characterises the Scottish VRU is virtually absent in England, compromising the hope of success for the initiative south of the border (JRF, 2015 (b); PPIW, 2015; National Audit Office blog, 2019). To frame an analogy: this is like buying a Formula 1 car and not employing a maintenance team on the racetrack. Sooner or later the car will stop working from lack of maintenance. That is not to say that multi-agency partnership working at the local level in England is not already in place. The author has wide experience of well-run and high-functioning multi-agency partnerships, but the Government-level support for this approach at national level has meant that local partnership working is daily shrivelling through lack of support and funding: in other words, the fuel for the initiative is leaking away. Local government officers who have hitherto provided administrative and corporate support for multi-agency partnerships are now so few that they cannot be spared from front line working to attend the meetings; resources are so scarce that funding for partnerships is all but gone at local level; cuts to police forces across the country have been so deep that officers cannot always spare the time away from the front line for partnership meetings. Here the author is referring to the need for a different approach to collaborative working and local multi-agency partnership. As a result of the lockdown for the global Covid19 pandemic in 2020, new ways of working have been clearly defined through online meetings (Bloomberg, 2020) and it may be that this can be continued to help sustain partnership working virtually at statutory and local levels. We must consider all legitimate and robust means for a new way of partnership working specifically to cut knife crime.

In spite of the public sector spending cuts and more recent difficulties in communication between partners due to Covid 19, co-ordinated efforts to stop knife crime are still required across all communities by statutory agencies, along with the Government, local authorities, police, voluntary sector, local people and others. It must be pointed out that a multi-strand, partnership approach is in fact specifically recommended in the British Government's Serious Violence Strategy published in 2018, (HM Government, 2018) in which an entire chapter is dedicated to the notion of partnership and collaborative working. Chapter five of the Strategy, 'Supporting Communities and Local Partnerships' argues that

> "Tackling serious violence requires a multiple strand approach involving a range of partners across different sectors and communities, and local partnerships are at the heart of this" (HM. Government, 2018, p.69).

The chapter goes on to argue that it is "essential" that Government helps local communities to tackle knife crime (p.69) yet this commitment is not matched by high-level government endorsement for local partnership working, much less to undertake partnership working with communities, as this book will demonstrate. After reviewing the evidence, we must begin to take a different view of supporting our local networks, communities and partnerships. Support is essential, and so too is commitment by the central and local government that this is a vital part of tackling knife crime. Government has a strong local voice through its local authorities and it should be strengthened to support the Serious Violence Strategy in its recommendations to tackle knife crime. It is true that our partnership working structure has been compromised due to reductions in funding to local government by central Government, but it can be achieved in spite of this.

Partnership and working together should now be redefined and reconstructed. To date, we in England have addressed multi-agency partnership through what are now outdated models. Committees of professionals meeting quarterly, under the guidance of the local authority and led by a politician and in which local issues are discussed will no longer be sufficient to deal with the complexity of knife crime. Partnership must be taken forward in a new way and on a much larger scale. Agencies should work together on a daily basis, across sectors in clearly defined geographic areas, networking virtually and in real time. Professionals and communities must create a different kind of partnership working: one that is dynamic, locally connected and most importantly, supported and funded by the government. This book explores how such a change might be achieved by learning lessons from those who do partnership best. Without a new, joint approach that supports partnership working, and a policy that puts partnership in the mainstream, more knife crime-related deaths are inevitable, as is greater fear of crime in society, and more families and communities devastated by the loss of a young life. A mother who had lost two sons to knife crime commented in a Guardian newspaper article called "I beg you to stop",

"I'm feeling pain. I can't sleep even, I can't sleep tonight," (The Guardian 22 February 2018 (a)).

Chapter 7

A new partnership working

In response to a question about how best to tackle knife crime, R: 18 (4 September, 2019) said that there is no single solution but that everyone should work together. R:18 is the former young offender whose life was turned around by the VRU approach in Glasgow after a stabbing incident on his front doorstep, as described above. He is an articulate and valued member of the VRU team now.

> "Absolutely. it's all the agencies like police, local government, social workers, you know? Everyone has to work together because it's never going to go away without that." (R:18. 4 September, 2019).

Additionally, one of the former prison officers interviewed for part of the longitudinal study added:

> "I agree with those guys in Scotland. You've got to work collaboratively, like with your partners and stuff. If we work together we might stand a chance of putting this right, you know? No one's got any resources now, so the only thing to do is work together. Well we've always done that and it works, you know? It really does." (R:11. 4 June, 2018)

Research for this book has shown that we must reimagine partnership working because constructing multi-agency groups in the ways that have gone before (HM Government, 1998; 2000 (a)) will not serve in the present crisis. Agency-led groups and partnerships with a local authority, politician or statutory body taking the lead will not address the diversity of the changing need. All too often, these partnerships are based on assembling a number of professionals that are usually already familiar to agencies where relationships have been built over time: partnerships must now re-think their composition and their dynamics. They must embrace virtual communities, special task groups, time-limited action, handing control to community organisations and leaders where appropriate, while encouraging new ways of engagement and functioning across sectoral boundaries and geographical areas. Those with the lived experience of knife crime should be involved in leading the way by chairing such partnerships where possible. In doing so, they can help to define the approach taken by statutory agencies in tackling violence, working with police, health professionals, schools and local government.

The author attended a multi-agency meeting in Hampshire intended to address youth violence and knife crime and to set up the local VRU and asked the question:" are there any young people here who have been involved in knife crime?" The answer came back that none were in attendance. The average age in the room was between 35 and 60. We must learn to include the people who can give us the most relevant information in our partnership and collaborative efforts. In addition, it is crucial that partnership must be adequately funded and resourced by the central and local government. In its absence, the approach cannot be properly co-ordinated or sustained over time. Things must change and this book explores the means by which it can happen.

Chapter 8

The project

Based on research undertaken by the author in 2018-19, and recent research in Glasgow, London, New York and evidence from Chicago in 2019, this book reconfigures earlier notions of collaborative leadership and partnership working by putting communities at the centre and community leaders in the forefront. It sets out how such an approach could work. It considers the way that a fully funded and well-resourced networking approach as in Glasgow has achieved clear results as demonstrated here. It reviews research undertaken in Chicago (Skogan, 2007), the Cure Violence and CeaseFire programmes at locations in the USA, the work of Police Scotland in Glasgow and services in London. Underlying this is a clear understanding that partnership must be redesigned in Britain to tackle the present rise in knife crime more effectively. This approach has not impacted knife crime successfully enough in the past and this is evidenced in the rising number of deaths in the UK. The old ways do not work any longer. We must begin to include the people who can most effectively help us to understand the problem, and this may involve working with perpetrators, offenders and victims. This is the view taken by the Scottish VRU and the USA's Cure Violence programme, as explained by R:2, (11 July, 2019) who argued,

> "..we can't set up an office and expect people to walk in and ask for our services. We have to go to them, using people they know and respect."

R:2 was clear in his assessment of what must happen to achieve a reduction in the kind of youth violence that we experience in Britain. Cure Violence in the USA is a programme based on the work of Dr Gary Slutkin whose work initiated the public health approach of the Scottish VRU to tackling community violence. Slutkin's ground-breaking public health approach to community violence comes from his experiences as an epidemiologist in Uganda and a recognition that the spread of violence in communities works in a similar way to epidemics and can be controlled through containment and intervention (Ransford and Slutkin, 2017; Roberts, 2019; HM Government and Public Health England, 2019). In short, treating violence as a public health issue is an idea that has been adopted by CeaseFire in the USA and the Scottish VRU, underpinning their ethos (SVRU, 2020). We shall explore the methods and ethos of Cure Violence further in the book. R:2 argued that violence in communities is a predictable phenomenon and can be tackled through understanding our communities and connecting with local intelligence. He stated that

> "Violence in communities is entirely predictable. Local communities know where the trouble spots and flashpoints are like parties, commemorations, events. All these things make violence predictable. This is the importance of knowing communities and staying in touch with them." (R:2. 11 July, 2019).

These insights are very significant. They echo the findings of Dr Gary Slutkin as shown above, in treating violence as an epidemic and public health issue. We can predict violence if we are familiar with our communities and engage with local intelligence. Such intelligence does not derive from a single source, however. It can come through various routes; statistics, locally gathered intelligence such as PCSO links to communities, and targeted enquiry. It is important to note that statistics can and do play a very significant role in predicting violence in localities. A paper by Massey, Sherman and Coupe (2019) discusses the ability of the Metropolitan Police Service (MPS) to pinpoint and predict where knife crime will occur in London. They found that by looking at non-fatal knife-enabled injuries over a 2-year period this can help pinpoint the future risk of homicide in local areas by up to 140%. This meant that were no specific 'hotspots' for repeated homicides, but there were such hotspots for non-fatal knife enabled injuries which helped predict the homicide risk in an area. Such information is helpful in allocating resources for the Metropolitan Police Service (MPS). Therefore, knowing or predicting the high-risk areas within communities, or in this case the geographical Lower Layer Super Output Areas (LSOA), would be vital (Gov.uk. 2020 (a)). LSOAs refer to census datasets and areas are defined as middle-range geographical datasets, (1500 people or 400 households). The way that we access this intelligence is key to responding to such predictions and the loss of some of our capacity to gain access to community intelligence has directly affected the ability to predict violence and therefore address it.

Over the ten years from 2010 -2020, we have lost a great deal of infrastructure which supports the provision of local intelligence, such as Police Community Support Officers(PCSOs), community policing, local youth workers, youth centres and clubs, community centres, social workers and many other resources (Roberts, 2019; Greig-Midlane, 2015; Loveday and Roberts, 2019). These losses will affect our ability to track and predict community violence.

> "Here we've seen reductions in police numbers that would make your eyes water and there are always going to be threats to the PCSOs because we're not warranted officers. The management always protect the

warranted officers. We're expendable. You've seen it in other parts of the country where they just get rid of us but you can bet your life, that community intelligence is what makes the differences between success and failure with detection and arrest." (R:16. 22 April, 2018)

Police Community Support Officers interact with local communities directly and support warranted police officers. Their work is not only deeply engaged with law enforcement and criminal justice, it is also directly related to the work of local authorities who have a key statutory role in community safety. Under section 17 of the 1998 Crime and Disorder Act, the duty on local authorities to consider the crime and disorder implications of all their day-to-day activities remains (HM Government, 1998). Ties with PCSOs are strong because of their direct involvement with communities with whom local authorities are daily engaged through service provision via the Youth Offending Services, Social Services, Hate Crime teams, Community Development, Youth Services, Housing, Education, Benefits and many more public services. Any cuts to funding, either to the police services or to local government will therefore impact the wider range of services adversely. To analyse these crucial elements of community violence and knife crime, we must therefore set a theoretical framework in place to enhance the robustness of the research.

Chapter 9

Research design

This research utilises the lived experience of those involved in knife crime for the purpose of identifying ways to tackle the violence. Lived experience derives from qualitative phenomenological research. Phenomenology is a philosophy which originated with Edmund Husserl (Giorgi and Giorgi, 2003) which tries to get to the truth of things by describing the phenomena as the individual experiences it (Moran, 2000. p.4). In simple words, things are described in a way that reflects individual experience because this is the reality for that individual. However, we take this notion further here, looking into the nuances offered by hermeneutic phenomenology and other theories that support the hypotheses.

The bedrock of the theoretical framework for the research behind this book is one of hermeneutic phenomenology but alongside this we will also consider the theory of Anomie (Husserl, 2001) and that of General Strain Theory (Agnew, 1992). The research methodology fits within the framework of lived experience because this research reviews the experience of individuals and their understanding of it. In this case, the discussion involves examining the experiences of perpetrators and victims, professionals and community representatives who have contributed to the book. The purpose of taking this approach is to reach a clearer understanding of solutions to the violence from the perspective of the victims, perpetrators, communities and professionals involved. These will constitute a new evidence base for proposed responses and solutions to knife crime.

Evidence-based solutions carry their own empirical power (alongside theoretical research). Fussey and Richards' 2008 paper identifies the lack of primary evidence in community violence. The value of such direct, primary research is that it directly addresses the need. We learn from victims, perpetrators, young offenders, police personnel, probation officers, social workers, community workers, community leaders, local authority personnel and third sector workers, all of whom provide their own immediate perspective. The clear advantage of this approach in using the evidence of shared individual and group experiences highlights a range of solutions rather than such reactive remedies as Stop and Search or increasing police officers on the street, which can only tackle single aspects of the violence. That is not to say that Stop and Search is not a valued part of the police response, or that police officers on the street should not be increased. Rather we need to consider the whole problem, not just aspects of it.

In addition, a co-ordinated structure of connective solutions are required and these are identified in this book through the actors involved, with special reference to those in Glasgow. They are also powerfully reflected in the current, highly successful Cure Violence approaches in some US cities and these will be explored within the research. It is argued that the strength of this shared experience provides evidence that there are proven, workable ways forward to address the issue of knife crime that we can learn from in Britain. However, this does not do away with the need for a strong theoretical framework to support the argument. Empirical research has its own theoretical bedrock, and this is explained below to help strengthen the research presented.

i) Theoretical framework

In accordance with the ontological perspective for this research, the significance of the shared effects of knife crime are demonstrated through examining the phenomenon from a variety of experiential perspectives. As explained, phenomenology lends itself to the research into knife crime because of the emphasis upon lived experience. In this chapter, phenomenology is also followed by Anomie (Durkheim, 2013) and General Strain Theory (Agnew, 1992). The latter explores the "strains" or pressures giving rise to criminal activity, making it relevant for our purposes in examining the context around knife crime. Adopting a very practical approach helps us identify solutions arising from the direct evidence of respondents. Anomie is explained below.

Phenomenological studies consider conscious experience from a subjective viewpoint. General Strain Theory (Agnew, 1992), suggests that the strains that people experience subjectively and collectively can result in extreme responses. Anomie describes the feelings and behaviours that accompany such individual and societal strains. The behavioural aspects of these strains can be observed and because of the empirical phenomena, it is possible to draw conclusions which can help us address knife crime in Britain. This highlights the value of this research to the academic discourse as the phenomenon of knife crime is explored through these actors. Therefore, those who have actually lived through such experiences, people who have endured the violence, those who have treated the victims, police personnel who try to address the issue through the criminal justice system, community workers, community leaders and local council employees who are tasked with tackling knife crime in local areas, are included.

ii) Phenomenology

Phenomenological research as a methodological approach, will be discussed with particular reference to hermeneutic phenomenology and transcendental phenomenology. There is a distinction between the two (Laverty, 2003. p.22; Creswell, 2007. p.59) which is worth noting as the focus in this book is on hermeneutic phenomenology. Before we examine the difference between the two, it is important to restate that phenomenology itself focuses on the value of lived experience as an empirical means of enquiry.

Edmund Husserl (1859-1938) is considered to be the father of phenomenology. His critique of research that focused only on the external world of stimuli, as experienced by individuals, was that it ignored the value of personal interpretation and the context of experience (Laverty, 2003. p.22). This represents a very significant insight, especially for the current research project. This is why phenomenology fits well with the study of knife crime, as the experience of the violence is most definitely interpreted by individuals and groups, and it is clearly shaped by context, as we will discover.

The value of Hermeneutic phenomenology lies specifically in the way that lived experience is shared in groups. Knife crime is not just experienced by individuals. It affects groups, neighbourhoods and communities too. There is now a large cohort of young people, their families, neighbours and friends who have experienced such violence, and from their joint lived experience, have been able to advance suggested remedies. The value of such solutions lies in the fact that these experiences are authentic and grounded in context. This will be explained here. Respondents have advocated a more joined-up, partnership approach to tackling the violence, greater use of individuals who have the lived experience of youth violence and knife crime in particular to help educate and intervene, better leadership for the initiatives that tackle knife crime within localities, a more holistic understanding of the problem by government and more sustained funding to support those fighting knife crime in communities.

With regard to the suggestion that we should deploy those involved, or those who have been involved in knife crime: people affected by youth and community violence report having more respect for those who have come from communities in which extreme violence is a regular occurrence and more readily accept interventions from those that they know have some understanding of their difficulties. R:18 (4 September, 2019) argued

> "I wouldn't have listened to someone who hadn't had the same experiences as me. You have to have people who understand. How can you help someone climb out of a hole if you haven't climbed out of it yourself?"

Here the respondent is referring to the "Navigators" who work for the Scottish Violence Reduction Unit (SVRU) in Glasgow and who spoke to him in hospital after the most recent of his many knife incidents. The SVRU uses a group of volunteers called Navigators who are front-line responders in hospitals and most importantly, have direct and personal experience of the crime. These are people from the local community who have shared similar experiences to the victims and are used by the SVRU to engage with the youngsters involved. It was one such Navigator who made the difference for R:18 as explained above.

The significance of that deep understanding through experience cannot be overstated. Applying remedies through people who have *not* undergone similar extreme experiences may only have a fairly nugatory effect upon those who are suffering its outcomes in some cases. But it is not always the case that direct experience of violence is essential.

The Ben Kinsella Trust in London (R22: 21 August 2019) provided a further insight into this phenomenon arguing that it is sometimes not essential to have someone with the same experiences, but rather that the intervener should be prepared to invest the time in the young person:

> "It's right to say that you have to use people who come from the same area, but I would say that although that authenticity is important, it's not absolutely crucial. Really, it's as much about someone being prepared to give these kids some time and talk to them: the building up of a relationship, that's important." (R:22. 21 August, 2019)

Merely having the same lived experience as someone else does not necessarily mean that person will make a good mentor, or Navigator. The SVRU trains its Navigators through a resourced programme in a similar way that the Cure Violence programme in the USA trains its recruits to interrupt the cycle of violence and support victims of gun and knife crime (CVG.org. 2020). Just having the lived experience is not sufficient to qualify people to become supporters, mentors or recruits to violence reduction programmes. As R: 22 argued, it is just as important to invest time in the young people involved in knife crime and this is why the training and support given to mentors, Navigators and Violence Interrupters is so important.

On the same theme, R2: (11 July 2019) argued that the Violence Interrupters must have their own credibility in the programme, but also supported the need for training to cope with potentially very violent situations. Cure Violence as a partnership-based organisation, relies on the training given to first responders in the community to defuse what R:2 called "the heat" from a violent situation.

"First of all, the violence interrupters are from the communities themselves. They have often done time and are well known. They have the credibility among communities, are known by everyone and are supported by Cure Violence. The workers are trained and paid ($30.000 a year) and have their own jackets or clothes with the Cure Violence i.d. on it. They go in unarmed." (R:2. 11 July, 2019).

Training and support is essential, and this requires funding and a commitment from those that hold the budget. Usually, this resides with government, and in the USA, with state government and mayors. Violence Interrupters are an essential element of the Cure Violence programme, representing the front line and first response. They are not sited within the Emergency Rooms (ERs) in America, as are the Navigators in the Scottish VRU, but are often situated within community centres or local hubs. R:2 describes the process which the Violence Interrupters go through and it is worth reproducing here:

"These guys go in unarmed and are trained to defuse a situation through a process.

1. Usually the perpetrator is "heated up" literally in the brain and requires what they call cooling down. This takes place with one of the workers.

2. They are in the grip of emotional hi-jack through the violence they have either witnessed or want to perpetrate. Interestingly, this is through community retaliation or through violence they have witnessed personally. Revenge is an issue and revenge to get respect. The thing is that these kids are often already traumatised through the system, like school or prison, or probation or some such. So they already have trauma through the system, then they experience trauma by violence. The code is peer pressure. Violence is bred through peer pressure.

3. The third party [Violence Interrupter] is necessary to help the perpetrator to literally cool down. They do this through

   a) Distraction – talking about something else

   b) Displacement – taking the person away from the situation

c) Cognitive dissonance – asking questions like what would your mother say about this? Or what would your teacher say if he could see what you're doing right now?

d) Mindfulness, being in the moment and activating the frontal lobe of the brain." (R:2. 11 July, 2019)

There is much to learn from this process; the 'heated up' condition of perpetrators in which violence seems the only response; the shared lived experience of the Violence Interrupters giving them the credibility; the process that they are trained to go through with perpetrators; the knowledge of the staged 'cooling down process' that needs to take place.

R:1 (13 July, 2019) is just such a Violence Interrupter. He is sited within a community hub on Staten Island in New York and through scanning social media and other local intelligence, "interrupts" or troubleshoots potential violence at source in neighbourhoods before it develops. A potentially dangerous, but very effective means of nipping youth violence in the bud, the Interrupters are highly valued in the Cure Violence programme as are the Navigators of the Scottish VRU. They work on a real front line in the streets and communities.

"But you see like I can go and do that because I'm known here, you know what I'm saying? These guys know me and they know I understand because I lived that life too." (R:1. 13 July, 2019)

This evidence perfectly describes the phenomenology referred to earlier; the connection between individual and shared experience, the importance of context, the interpretation of experiences by the individuals. From this essential resource it is possible to glean information about why youth violence happens, what triggers it, what it feels like to enact it and what the potential solutions might be. From observing and participating in the phenomenon, the solutions become evident and one of the most obvious is that engaging with the violence on the front line through those involved is key to addressing it.

iii) Background to phenomenology

In general, phenomenology relates to the reality experienced by people rather than exploring abstract philosophical concepts. This is important in the context of this research which seeks to provide evidence-based solutions to knife crime. As shown above, there is an irrefutable power in evidence taken from lived experience, and the solutions suggested are powerful because of this evidence. The review and evaluation of existing works, exploring abstract concepts to deduce a range of conclusions in the author's view can support the strength of experiential evidence. Being able to say 'I know this because I have experienced it' can carry as much weight as saying 'I know this because I have read about it': perhaps more. That is not to say one is less valid than the other: simply that knife crime as a phenomenon is now at such critical proportions that it seems sensible to suggest a response that is more holistic. This could be seen as a subjective judgement on the part of the author. Nonetheless, in a world in which we are grappling with a reality that means life or death for so many people, it seems logical in this instance to apply equal value to the evidence of those with experience.

Yet it must be said that we do not only learn through lived experience. For the purpose of finding a way forward in resolving the issue of knife crime in Britain, the author contends that insufficient attention has been given to this aspect of the phenomenon. In the past, we have tended to try to think our way out of the problem with little recourse to those who could help us in to apply lived experience to these problems: those who are affected by knife crime and those who are involved in communities. Previously, we have concentrated on looking at the causes, not the possible solutions. Phenomenology helps us to consider both.

iv) The philosophical background

As briefly mentioned earlier, Edmund Husserl (1859-1938) is considered the founder of phenomenology which refers to the study of individual experience in the world. It is important to state that Husserl considered that such experience cannot be separated from the individual but is an essential part of that person. Husserl's phenomenology represented a movement away from the old ways of thinking in terms of Cartesian dualism (Thibaut, 2018) in that the mind and body are not separate in phenomenology because personal experiences are comprised of both minds and bodies (Laverty 2003, p.23). It was French philosopher Descartes (1641) that defined the so-called mind-body split, in terms of separating the thinking entity from the physical one. Mind and body were considered in isolation. Phenomenology draws the two back together so that experience becomes something that happens to the individual and something that people are capable of processing, assimilating and considering through both their minds and their bodies.

v) Transcendental phenomenology

The emphasis, in transcendental phenomenology, is on the individual and his or her experience as it appears to them (Warren and Wakefield, 2016). This is intended to help discover the nature of things in essence: to arrive at a purity of understanding. The focus is still upon lived experience in transcendental phenomenology, but the expectation is that we have the ability to reflect upon experience in order to discover meaning through contemplating the essential nature of that experience. It is almost a meditational exercise. This was the Husserlian foundation of phenomenology, but particular reference will be made now to the later iteration of phenomenology by the German philosopher, Martin Heidegger (1889 - 1976). Husserl had little interest in the emotional connotations of experience, but this lack of interest seems to sideline one of the key features of human experience, and certainly one that features strongly in knife crime. Our emotions often shape and colour our response to our experiences and relate to the context around them, as we saw with the description of the Violence Interrupters above. R:2 (19 July, 2019) referred to a situation in which perpetrators are literally "heated up" or emotionally hijacked by involvement in the violence. Emotions play a strong role in youth and community violence. However, later developments in the study of phenomenology took matters further towards Hermeneutics.

vi) Hermeneutic phenomenology

What makes hermeneutic phenomenology important for this research is that it looks at the meaning of shared, lived experience for individuals and groups (Creswell, 2007 p.57). Knife crime, although perpetrated against individuals, has now become a shared experience in which groups of perpetrators, victims and communities relate to the trauma, loss and consequences of knife crime. It has become an experience that connects people. In that sense, it describes hermeneutic phenomenology (Husserl, 1900) which attempts to interpret the meaning of experience, not so much to develop a composite understanding of the experiences, but to identify the connections between them (James, 2018). It is a tragedy that these connections are often trauma, shock and bereavement for groups and communities as well as the affected individuals in families.

For the purpose of this research, we will align hermeneutic phenomenology with the "radical empiricism" of James (cited in Moran, 2000 p.14). This is an important distinction because James emphasised the 'particulars' of experience and the connections between those particulars. The connectedness of the experiences of knife crime, the particulars of joint feelings of tragedy and bereavement examined in this book are central to the formulation of possible solutions as suggested by respondents. This is because patterns of responses can be determined, especially in the universal call for all agencies to work together better to tackle knife crime, and in enabling us to define a way forward based on empirical evidence. Moreover, this empirical evidence has the strength of numbers behind it. For example, here we are not presenting a single individual with experience of knife crime, but rather many individuals with a shared experience of it.

"I can't never forget this. I watched him die. I can't forget it; not me, not my family, not no one I know." (R:14. 12 June, 2018)

"Well, you can only really have one view, can't you, if you're human. It's an absolute tragedy for the kids and their families, and for society" (R:8. 20 June, 2018)

All victims interviewed for this project described the effects upon the whole community in similar ways. One death of a youngster in a community will affect the family, friends, loved ones and local people throughout the area. National reporting and news media will bring these deaths to the attention of a national and international audience. The connective ripples of knife crime homicide can be seen everywhere.

This is linked to the choice of phenomenology for this research. Where Husserl began to break new ground in developing phenomenology was through highlighting the significance of joint or shared experience between individuals. This was explored more deeply later by Heidegger. In Husserl's work, he identified the fact that psychology had hitherto relied upon the methods from the natural sciences to interpret and examine behaviour. Our subjects, as with Husserl's observation, are human beings who do not automatically react to external stimuli but have the ability to reflect upon and interpret experiences autonomously.

The variables which Husserl felt had been missed were context and interpretation on the part of the individual (Laverty, 2003). While these are important, we must distil (Creswell, 2007 p.58) shared experiences and emotional responses to explore the essence of them to interpret their meaning and what they have in common, to help identify solutions to knife crime.

As explained above, hermeneutic phenomenology was later developed by German philosopher Martin Heidegger (1889-1976), who worked with Husserl but in later years, distanced himself from Husserl's work. The emphasis for Heidegger was also on lived experience but he took this further. He focused on the way such experience is interpreted by individuals as they exist in the world – which for Heidegger meant literally a way of being in the world, or 'Dasein' (Heidegger, 2010 p.15). This 'being in the world' situates experiences as part of individual reality, and as such makes the interpretation of that experience relatable to the phenomenon of knife crime in modern society. The individual will filter his or her experience through a mesh of emotion and context, both of which will be peculiar to that individual. Whilst we do not need a lengthy exposition of Heidegger's treatise "Being and Time"(1953) in which being-in-the-world or Dasein is explored, what concerns us here is the emphasis on the interpretation and meaning of experience for people. More relevant to this research is that Laverty, in her 2003 work, pointed out that Heidegger emphasised the salience of <u>context</u> within individual understanding (2003, p.24). Furthermore, the notion of context, or what Heidegger calls 'pre-understanding', cannot be considered separately from people's experience. With knife crime, this is a crucial insight and the very crux of the need to recognise hermeneutic phenomenology as one of the most suitable methodological approaches for this research. The context around knife crime can be seen as the primary element of the issue, as explored below. Context is studied in this book through the lives of affected individuals who grow up in difficult circumstances, experience neglect and trauma in their early lives, go through school where life is full of difficulty and challenge, get involved in gangs or violence or both, go to prison or perpetrate violence. Context is vital to understanding knife crime and routes out of it. This is recognised in Government both here in the UK, the USA and further afield.

In the British Government's Serious Violence Strategy (HM Government, 2018) the lived experience of knife crime is bound up in the social context of poverty, deprivation, childhood trauma, exposure to neighbourhood and personal violence. These describe the settings in which knife crime thrives and the individual cannot be separated from it. The way that people commonly understand and interpret their experiences, share them and connect them to others defines the phenomenon of knife crime in England. This context clearly includes poverty, deprivation, adverse childhood experiences or ACES, lack of housing, trauma, worklessness and poor access to education. But the shared experience of knife crime can at the same time offer us solutions. From evidence provided by respondents to this research, we can link the patterns denoted through the causes shown above and define the ways in which respondents have forged a response. Examples of this would be emphasising the validity of experiential understanding in those trying to support the victims of knife crime; utilising those with lived experience to work with perpetrators and others to stop the violence; partnering with the police and other agencies to work with children in schools to help educate them about the dangers and effects of knife-carrying; including those with experience of knife crime in multi-agency partnership working and 'front line' services in hospitals to help inform responses. To some extent, this happens with the Violence Interrupters in the USA's Cure Violence programme and the SVRU's Navigators in Glasgow. The value of proposed solutions from those involved with the problems should not be ignored.

vii) Finer details of phenomenology

James (2018) was at pains to explain that radical empiricism includes meaning, intentionality and values: all of which will be examined in this book. We will explore the meanings behind knife crime, the values driving gang violence the intentionality (or the way an act is directed towards something), and how we can address these elements. At this point, it is worth re-defining intentionality in the classical, Husserlian context.

Our own experiences are directed towards (through intention) something only through various concepts, ideas, values and meanings that are peculiar to us. This is important when considering knife crime because stabbings are perpetrated against the individual and are influenced by the societal conditions, ideas, impressions, contexts and values around those involved. Knife crime does not happen without context. Sanders McDonagh's work with young offenders refers to this where she argued:

> "Most of the young men I've spoken to grew up in areas with high levels of deprivation with disproportionately high levels of violent crime compared to other areas of London. One young man started carrying a knife at the age of 12, as he was afraid to walk across his estate to and from school" (Sanders-McDonagh, 2019).

As expressed by commentators (Roberts, 2019; Sanders-McDonagh, 2019), knife crime happens for many complex reasons. There are experiential commonalities and contextual factors in terms of deprivation, poverty, repeated early life trauma, drug and gang-related violence not just here in the UK but in other countries (HM Government, 2018; Leovy, 2015; Sanders-McDonagh, 2019; Roberts, 2019). It is the phenomenological connections, expressed in terms of those commonalities and manifested in communities, which concern us here.

To be clear, we are referring to the experience of knife crime on the part of victims, perpetrators, parents, communities, statutory agencies, police, charities and others. It is not the intention here to re-examine the causes, but to analyse shared experience to find answers. For example, do victims, perpetrators, parents, communities and others all have an idea of how to resolve this crisis? The answer is that they do have a shared idea and for many, the response is the same. Not one respondent in the whole range disagreed that the means to resolve this lies in people and agencies working together collaboratively: not in the old ways, but in more subtle, nuanced ways. The author is aware that positionality is an issue here in that the questions asked of respondents will have shaped the research in many ways. For example, there is no representative from a white, working-class background, no party-political view, no inclusion of elite professionals in the sample. The scope of the research is such that the premise underpinning it is that people involved in knife crime at all levels are best placed to help find solutions. This is based on research undertaken in 2018 and 2019 in which respondents began to articulate opinions and conclusions about the way in which we as policy makers, politicians, academics, citizens and professionals could respond differently to knife crime to help tackle its growth in society (Roberts, 2019).

It is clear from the research undertaken for this book that there is no substitute, no proxy for the lived experience of knife crime. From its manifestation as an experience we can distil the ways in which the phenomenon can be addressed both from communities and from individuals. As expressed by R: 18 (4 September, 2019),

> "It's the lived experience of knife crime that matters here, especially in communities. There's no substitute for it and no credibility without it when you're looking for solutions."

The need for such credibility was echoed by R: 1 (13 July, 2019) in Staten Island

> "You can't use people who don't understand. That ain't going to work. You have to have people who've lived it, right? You can't use outsiders. You have to use the people who know the community, have been through what these guys have been through, understand the trauma and have the local links and the relationships."

This is a well-recognised approach and is one used both by the Scottish VRU and the Cure Violence programme in the USA. Credibility matters when engaging with those involved in the violence and when trying to effect solutions and remedies. Credibility and lived experience is further explored within this book as part of the response to reducing knife crime.

viii) Anomie and General Strain Theory

A second strand to the theoretical framework for this book are the notions of Anomie (Durkheim, 2013) and Strain Theory, (Agnew 1992). Anomie describes the societal context which can give rise to the "deregulation and disintegration" of society (Teymoori, Bastian and Jetten, 2017). Anomie, originally framed by Durkheim in his 1897 book, "The Division of Labour in Society" describes a reduced state of society in which the individual may experience the destruction of social integration and regulation. From here comes a withdrawal from civic engagement, a sense of alienation from the norms of society, feelings of helplessness and meaninglessness. Skogan, Hartnett, Bump and Dubois (2008) refer to these norms in their analysis of the success of the Cure Violence and CeaseFire programmes in the USA to tackle community violence. Norms, they argue, are beliefs, values and attitudes that constitute the culture of a community (p.8). The absence of these norms, Durkheim argues, comes from feelings that the regulation or governance of society has failed us. Where Anomie refers to the failure of social integration and regulation, it includes "collective responses and collective perceptions" (Teymoori, Bastian and Jetten, 2017 p. 1011). Those responsible for Anomie are held to be those who construct the policies that regulate society: namely, the state or Government. This is an important insight when considering knife crime. Merton (1938;1968) crucially pointed out that those in lower socio-economic groups tend to experience anomie in the sense described above. It must therefore be noted that knife crime thrives in areas where inequality is rife; where those experiencing poverty, deprivation and hopelessness on a daily basis live their lives.

Strain Theories propose that certain stressors such as those described above, increase the likelihood of crime (Agnew and Scheuerman, 2014). These stressors can precipitate the expression of anger and frustration which may result in perceived "corrective" or revenge action through violence. This is a well-documented element of knife crime (The Independent, (b) June 2019; Wood, 2010, p.11; The Guardian, (c) 2018; Sanders-McDonagh, 2019).

Emile Durkheim (1858-1917) developed the first coherent Strain Theory, setting out the link between Anomie and deviant behaviour in his 1893 book, The Division of Labour in Society (Durkheim, 2013). Durkheim referred to a condition or state (Teymoori, Bastian and Jetten, 2017. p.1009) in wider society in which he describes a kind of social disintegration which is Anomie. This occurs when the norms and regulatory framework of society become lost so that individuals no longer know what to expect from each other. Society therefore becomes anomic when we lose sight of how to treat each other. Crucially, the state of Anomie exists in the "interface" between the individual and society (Teymoori, Bastian and Jetten, 2017). This is important when considering knife crime due to the feelings often expressed by respondents for this study about the disconnection between the state and individuals in society.

IV "Look, its like, no one gives a shit no more. Not police, not no one.

SR Why do think no one gives a shit?

IV Because that's how it is man! Like – life here it ain't nothing like what you got man. You don't know nothing." (R:14. 12 June, 2018)

The young man who expressed these feelings was by no means untypical of those involved in the interviews and was reflected in the law enforcement agencies who participated in this research. A former prison officer from London Pentonville argued that the youngsters

> "......know the police don't come out any more, they know there's no sanction for what they're doing to each other. I mean, they've seen everything go haven't they, and Grenfell didn't help. It just brought out all the divisions. Kids feel like they've been pushed out onto the streets – treated like they don't belong." (R:28. 4 June, 2018)

The connection between Anomie and higher levels of crime is made in Durkheim's Division of Labour in Society (2013). Broad socio-structural change, such as that experienced in Britain since 2010 and the introduction of Austerity by the Coalition Government in 2010 is a catalyst for anomie if those changes are considered to be negative (Teymoori, Bastian and Jetten, 2017). Warnings about the risks of such a policy were pointed out early on (Taylor-Gooby, 2012 p.66), especially among the most vulnerable in society. Moreover, their effects upon the poor and disenfranchised were deplored by Sir Philip Alston, the United Nations' special rapporteur on poverty (OFCHR, 2018) when he visited Britain in 2018. The statement he issued described an anomic society in the most explicit Durkheimian terms.

> "It thus seems patently unjust and contrary to British values that so many people are living in poverty. This is obvious to anyone who opens their eyes to see the immense growth in foodbanks and the queues waiting outside them, the people sleeping rough in the streets, the growth of homelessness, the sense of deep despair that leads even the Government to appoint a Minister for suicide prevention and civil society to report in depth on unheard of levels of loneliness and isolation. And local authorities, especially in England, which perform vital roles in providing a real social safety net have been gutted by a series of government policies." (OFCHR, 2018).

In Alston's statement, it is worth noting his emphasis on the loss of local services which provide the "safety net" for individuals who are struggling in society. The loss of this safety net is described as a direct result of the Austerity policy inaugurated by the Coalition Government (The Guardian, (b) 2018; IPPR, 2019; Oxfam, 2013; JRF, 2015 (b)) and is echoed by R: 28 (4 June, 2018).

> "I know so many [children] who have lived like sofa surfing, out on the streets, homeless. There's no way they can afford a place in London and the housing benefit they get now is way too small. They can't pay for a room even if they could find one. It's actually mad isn't it. When you look

at housing in London. No one can afford it. Who are all these guys who come into to London and buy up all the flats and let them at like crazy prices? I'll tell you this for nothing, no kid I know is going to afford one of those. In fact, no one can afford them unless you earn like stupid money" (R:28. 4 June 2018)

Anomie has been linked to psycho-social outcomes such as "alienation, meaninglessness, helplessness or confusion" (Teymoori, Bastian and Jetten, 2017 p. 1011). Anomie accurately describes a modern, disintegrated British society and the development of the knife crime epidemic can be connected with it (YMCA, 2020; Huffington Post, 2018). This was a Government policy decision which has dismantled large sections of social welfare and the protections it provides for those most vulnerable in modern British society. The resentment which results from perceived injustices on the part of the state can be seen in the knife crime issue. Young people openly resent the loss of housing benefit for young single men (Roberts, 2019) the ending of the Education Maintenance Allowance in England (Gov.uk, 2020 (a)) the loss of benefits through Universal Credit, the removal of local services such as youth support services among others. Many of these services are administered or provided by local authorities who have been so badly affected by public sector cuts by the central government. It has not escaped young people's attention that the state has virtually abandoned local areas, particularly in London.

"I mean have you even seen where we live man? Have you even seen? It's like you wouldn't give it to your dog man. Place is like filthy you know? And no one even cares nothing about us, or what we do or where we go like" (R:14. 12 June, 2018)

Anomie also refers to shared perceptions of context (Teymoori, Bastian and Jetten, 2017. p.1011) and this links closely with the notion of Hermeneutic Phenomenology as described above. Context is of central importance and group perceptions of context often shape the response to a crisis or feeling of injustice in society. Just as important are the explicit connections between these feelings (James, W. cited in Moran, 2000. p.14) which are shared among individuals experiencing a trauma such as knife crime. Feelings are characterised by a sense of dislocation from a society that no longer cares enough to enforce its own rules; emotions such as resentment against the state; a mood of self-reliance and self-determination often manifesting as the freedom to "make our own rules" (R:6. 18 July, 2018); a palpable feeling of fear and abandonment.

"......it's like when the police left around here, or I mean when there weren't no police like, kids like thought, right, they've gone so we can do what we like innit? And they like do." (R:6. 18 July, 2018)

The welfare of citizens at the most vulnerable end of society appears to many respondents in this research to no longer be a concern for government. Young people feel that state and police have left them to their own devices. Without sanctions, they feel that it no longer matters to either government or police that extreme violence and knife-carrying is now a way of life for them. Low police numbers represent a "window of opportunity" (Roberts, 2019) for those seeking to perpetrate violence against others. It is essential, therefore, that welfare becomes a focus for the government and the gaps in provision must be addressed as a matter of greatest urgency. This manifestation of Anomie can be reversed.

ix) Strain Theory

During the 1940s, Robert K. Merton utilised Durkheim's term Anomie to develop a theory of deviance which became known as Strain Theory. Rising crime in America prompted this development. In seeking an explanation for crime rates, Merton pointed out that in spite of the aims of the American dream in which individuals could succeed whatever their background or social origin, not everyone has achieved it (Thompson, 2016). The tension between this ideal and the reality creates "strain" for the individual and in the face of such pressure to achieve material success, some individuals turn to illegitimate means for achieving it. Merton's theory was that a criminal response to the inability to achieve the ideal American Dream derives from those who are part of the lower socio-economic groups and the unskilled. In the present study, however, the evidence suggests that the current knife crime epidemic in Britain does not necessarily originate among the "unskilled" but rather among the disenfranchised. The criminal response to "strain" may well arise from a lack of good housing, low educational achievement, deprivation, impoverishment and desperation of some groups in society. Yet it does not necessarily equate to ignorance or lack of skill. In many cases, the young people who were part of this research were intelligent, socially aware individuals displaying a wide variety of untapped skill. Many were, however, victims of adverse childhood experiences such as abuse and negligence and most had struggled with deprivation and poverty or been bullied and victimised at school. Some had been misdiagnosed with ADHD (Attention Deficit Hyperactivity Disorder) and sent to a Pupil Referral Unit (PRU) where they encountered drug dealing and grooming by gangs. Some went on to become part of the County Lines drugs network in Britain. Others had endured hardship and poverty in their early lives. This did not indicate a lack of intelligence or skill. What was much more evident was the sense of hopelessness and helplessness which these youngsters manifested, and which will become evident through their voices represented here.

Strain Theory gives us an insight into the notion of the "haves and have-nots" where much resentment against the state originates. In a group interview undertaken for this research, two youngsters spoke to the author about this perceived gap.

> "...people like you, you need to get it that there's the way you live, right, and then there's the way we live and it's not like right, you know? Why do we like have this to live with and you don't?
>
> Res1: No, you can't say that. It's not her fault is it.
>
> Res5. Yes it is. It's all of her type and people like her." (R:6. 30 July, 2018)

The inequality highlighted by Merton showed that in America, where many felt that society valued and promoted goals that were largely unachievable, being unable to attain the American Dream legitimately prompted young people to try to achieve it illegitimately through crime. This is a key observation because it is evident from much of the discourse around knife crime that British youngsters appear to feel that they are the victims of the unattainable: that there is such a gap between the haves and have nots in society that they will never achieve material wealth unless through crime, such as drug dealing. This young man argued:

> "I just want to have a decent life. You know, a wife, a family a decent car. Not nothing big. Just to be normal. It's like impossible. No one can help me. They never have." (R: 7. 9 November, 2018 and 31 July, 2019).

The former prison officer from London Pentonville echoed the evidence of R7: above.

> "But look, don't get me wrong. They're not all involved in it and I've worked with loads of kids who just want a decent life. Look, when you ask them, what they want, it's really sad because they say stuff like a nice house and a car. Not like millions of pounds or stuff. It's really ordinary things they want, maybe things we'd take for granted." (R: 28. 4 June, 2018)

The author attended a Serious Violence Summit organised by Southampton City Council in February 2020. Here a report of a young girl was shared in which she had become involved in dealing drugs and was making £1,000 a week. At

15, she was more concerned about where to keep her cash than her own safety or the safety of those affected by her illegal activities. To ensure her cash wealth was secure, she put herself into care (R:25. 6 February, 2020) early in 2020. She desperately wanted to be financially secure but the illegitimate means of securing such stability frightened her to the extent that she feared for her life, seeking the security of a family life to protect her from the perceived and probably very real threat that she would be targeted because of her money.

The relevance of Strain Theory (Agnew, 1992) here is that it is created at a socio-psychological level focusing on individuals in their immediate environment or context (p.48). This links strongly with phenomenology and the notion that context, and strain, are significant (Laverty, 2003) in the proliferation of violence. The focus for Agnew in his work was upon adolescents, and many of the victims and perpetrators of knife crime in Britain are indeed adolescents. This, alongside the recognition that adverse experiences affect certain individuals, makes General Strain Theory and phenomenology relevant for this study. Both recognise that the connections between individuals and groups can influence behaviour in the empirical world and that context is highly significant.

Agnew (1992) emphasises that strain theory focuses on what he terms "negative relationships with others" (p.48), going on to define this as the individual not being treated as they would wish. This is a trope that emerges regularly in the interviews for this research in that young people feel they have not been treated either fairly or justly, perhaps by their peers, by the police or by the wider state. Agnew (1992; 2014) highlights the fact that not all those experiencing stressors turn to violence. Yet as will be shown in this research, repeated stressors, or what R:1 called "Trauma, on top of trauma, on top of trauma" renders the individual more likely to respond to such stressors with violence. In fact, many knife-related offences are often experienced as revenge attacks, fuelling an escalation of knife crime. Staff in the Scottish Violence Reduction Unit in Glasgow affirmed that this experience of repeated trauma must be taken into account when trying to address knife crime

> "The context in terms of deprivation, repeated trauma and adverse childhood experiences are all major influences in knife crime." (R: 21. 4 September, 2019)

It must be recognised that General Strain Theory (GST), (Agnew,1992) is most relevant for this study because it focuses on societal and individual strains such as the inability to achieve goals, the loss of valued possessions and negative or violent treatment by others. These are features that are treated by Durkheim in describing Anomie. Again, these foci are reflected in the UK Government's

Serious Violence Strategy (HM Government, 2018). The latter is particularly relevant, as shown in the evidence from respondents in the research. Agnew and Scheuerman (2014) reveal evidence which points to the fact that the strains evident in GST increase the likelihood of crime.

The key message from these two theories; Hermeneutic Phenomenology and General Strain Theory, is that both context and trauma (stressors) combine in the knife crime phenomenon to create the increased likelihood of offending and becoming a victim. This perpetuates the cycle of knife-related violence currently witnessed in Britain. This is supported by evidence identified in the Serious Violence Strategy (HM Government, 2018) in which is it acknowledged that Adverse Childhood Experiences (ACES), poverty, deprivation, domestic violence, low educational attainment, unemployment and poor health are strong "predictors" for serious violence (pp.36-37). These stressors, strains and experiences provide the context or backdrop for knife crime which often proliferates by way of gangs in the UK which are explored in this book.

Chapter 10

History of the research

In 2018, the author undertook a nine-month project researching knife crime in London, reviewing its causes and proposed solutions put forward by those who participated in the project. This was published in early 2019 (Roberts, 2019). Further research has been added to that undertaken in 2018, including interviews with those who lead the response to youth and community violence in the USA, London and Glasgow. These new interviews included actors involved in leading the Cure Violence programme in Chicago and New York, front line workers in the Cure Violence initiative in New York, police and local authority personnel in Glasgow and the Metropolitan police in London. In addition, the author interviewed more youth leaders and community professionals living and working in London, Glasgow and New York. Previously unpublished primary evidence from those interviewed in 2018 have also been included in this book.

The reason for including new research is to review and explore some of the solutions that have been shown to work in combating youth and community violence. Knife crime in Britain is now such a complicated and embedded issue that our thoughts must be focused on its many facets to refocus attention from punitive criminal justice measures and more police and punishment towards a holistic approach. It is essential that this includes the rest of society as a whole. As a societal issue, it must be expected that we should all be involved in effecting solutions to the current crisis.

i) Research for this study and "wicked problems"

Primary research of the type used in this study is a necessary part of any attempt to find effective solutions to highly complex, or "wicked" problems (Rittel and Webber, 1973). It helps to provide a nuanced approach, enabling a close examination of the variables in such complicated societal issues. A wicked problem of the type discussed by Rittel and Webber (1973) is an intricate one, existing at many different levels. It can be the case with such wicked problems, having many complicated interdependencies, that solving one aspect may reveal a variety of other problems. The connectedness (James, 2018) referred to earlier in relation to phenomenology is important here. Such is the case with knife crime in Britain at this time: things happen for many reasons. It is not a case of simply losing 20,000 police officers or cuts to local government services (Roberts, 2019); not merely problems of social cohesion or issues of racism; not just the complicated issues around housing or gangs and postcode warfare in cities. It has much more to do with the connectedness of these issues. It is probably correct to say that no issue in society exists in isolation. This is very much the case with knife crime. Moreover, it can be exacerbated by the individualist nature of modern society and the way successive British governments have historically tackled social issues in piecemeal, isolated chunks of time with time-limited funding. The roots of the violence, the attitudes towards it and the enactment of it are all connected to issues. These range from school exclusion to mental health; from poverty to deprivation and neglect; from the loss of police personnel to cuts in youth clubs and community centres; from the rise in social media use to online gaming, social media bullying, loneliness and isolation. All are key variables within this tragic issue.

ii) Knife crime now

Knife crime and community violence are now at record high levels (The Independent, July 2019 (b); The Telegraph, April 2019; BBC News, 18 July 2019; House of Commons Library, 2018). It is important to now look beyond the manifestations of the problem to some of the many issues that lie in the context of knife crime to help us look onwards for ideas to resolve this complicated problem. Gone are the days when professionals and politicians can opine their way out of societal ills. It will no longer serve our purposes to simply consult those who deal with the violence on a professional level such as social workers, teachers, local authority community safety personnel, police and youth workers to tell us what the problems are. We must ask those involved in the violence to help us find a way forward.

Immediate recourse to the professionals for answers to social issues is an approach that some local authorities have habitually taken over the years. The author has worked in local and national government for many years, witnessing many occasionally gauche attempts to address social issues by asking the professionals rather than the people involved. For example, the author once asked a local government elected member if members of the public as local taxpayers could be invited to attend a planning meeting for the council budget. The (elderly male) elected member said "Don't be ridiculous! You'll have them taking all the money!".

Our methods must be changed. Our means of gathering information about social issues must be informed by those who are involved, not through soliciting the opinions of those who hold the purse strings. Primary research is therefore the most appropriate and the most accurate means of finding out how best to tackle knife crime.

iii) Why we must re-establish links with communities

With regard to the findings for this research project: one of the most important areas to address with regard to knife crime is that of re-establishing closer links with communities. In Britain, it is clear that after the loss of many local government workers, police and community safety staff, working with communities has become much more difficult without the granularity of neighbourhood intelligence in a locality. Public sector workers have close ties with communities and individuals such as PCSOs, youth workers, social workers or community leaders can provide vital links to support services. But these have been adversely affected by the reduction in police numbers, the closure of community centres and youth clubs and the reduced numbers of PCSOs (Roberts, 2019). Vital links to communities and community intelligence are therefore being lost. O'Neill, (2014) describes the key importance of the connective role that PCSOs have in their areas and the kinds of agencies that they are able to connect people to (p.269). She talks about the strength of the local knowledge that PCSOs can build and their ability to develop sustained social capital in communities (O'Neill, 2014. p.269). The loss of such connectivity can be devastating in terms of both the social cohesion in an area and the partnership working which is so vital in tackling youth violence. In describing the work of the PCSOs, she refers to the linked agencies and individuals who work collaboratively in local areas.

"This will include not only local residents, but also other public sector agency workers in the area (such as youth workers, anti-social behaviour teams, and local counsellors); shop workers and owners; and private sector services and staff (such as housing providers and security staff). All of these networks and links are utilized regularly to address problems in an area, to gather intelligence for police colleagues." (O'Neill, 2014. p.269)

The loss of just one of the local links in this community chain of partners, such as a PCSO, community development or youth worker can mean a tangible gap in local intelligence which can inhibit the ability of the police to tackle serious violence in the form of knife crime. Vibrant, high functioning community intelligence can make the difference between effectively addressing this problem and failing to stop it. Re-establishing links with communities is therefore essential.

Research undertaken by the author during 2018 and 2019 has elicited some relevant insights. These insights include opinions from communities and individuals about the causes of knife crime and the views of both those involved and the professionals about how to resolve it. Such comments also relate to the way that people now regard their sense of community, feelings of belonging, cohesion, mutual understanding and tolerance. Some of these comments are difficult to read, and the voices of young people in pain are hard to hear. Many of these comments reflect an Anomic society in which people feel isolated, alienated, hopeless and helpless (Teymoori, Bastian and Jetten, 2017. p.1011). The evidence from young people here represents a real cry from the heart offering up a genuine plea for a restored sense of community.

This young person was part of a group interview which took place in 2018 for research into knife crime. He commented on the community in which he lives, and was answering a question about how we need to tackle the violence, arguing that

> "You need everything, like everyone, you know? It's not just no police and stuff, it's everything, like we said. It's people like [youth worker's name] working with us and talking to us, and police, and somewhere to go. It's not going to be quick, like, you know – send in a few police and stop them. It's more than all that." (R: 6. 30 July, 2018)

There are hints within the above comment about not having anywhere to go and meet friends, the loss of communication with statutory agencies like the police, via PCSOs; having no one to talk to about their issues; knowing that the damage is so extensive in communities that putting things right is "not going to be quick, like, you know."

A further respondent commented about the lack of hope on his return to the community after his release from prison, stating in response to the author's question about why he got involved in County Lines drugs dealing:

> R: All my friends they're doing it so I would be like the odd one out like. You just do it because there's nothing else. I mean like really nothing. What have I got? Like no GCSEs man, no qualifications. Nothing.

> SR: Was there nothing offered to you in prison?

> R: (Laughs) What you think it's like some kind of charity thing in there man. You're joking ain't you? I got offered weed, Spice, that kind of stuff. Not qualifications man. I got a job the last month before I got out on licence working in the kitchens. That's it.

> SR: That's terrible. So you've come out with nothing

> R: I come out with like a drugs habit man. (R: 7. 9 November, 2018)

His comments are reflected by others speaking about communities, particularly this youth worker in Croydon who argued:

> "what I want to say is: it's been coming a long time. You can see the seeds of this when we started losing youth centres, community workers and places for kids to go. What did they think would happen when they took these things away from kids? Honestly, if they've got nowhere to go and no one to help them, well the whole thing is just a powder keg in London." (R:8. 20 June, 2018)

In response, it is essential to ask questions about what could have happened in London and elsewhere that has contributed to the disintegration of community networks and support? Put more simply, what is it that has been lost to communities? It is certainly true to say that local support services have been cut as part of the Coalition, then Conservative Government's policy of Austerity (Roberts, 2019; Hastings, et.al. 2015; Institute for Fiscal Studies, 2017; Alston, 2018; Clayton, Donovan and Merchant, 2015). These services are part of the wide range of provision led by local authorities in Britain and youth services have been cut across the country. In fact, youth services such as clubs and youth support have been "massively" cut since 2010, alongside the general programme of retracting public services (Youdell and McGimpsey, 2014. p.122). This is important because local service delivery, under the aegis of local government, is part of the safety net for youngsters in towns, cities and villages across Britain. These losses are significant and we will see why here.

Chapter 11

Loss of youth services

UNISON issued a report in 2019 saying that between 2010 and 2019, youth services have lost £400 million in cuts (UNISON, 2019.). The same report details the losses in terms of both funding and youth centres, with 763 closing over the 9 years covered by the report. This represents a loss to young people of safe spaces to go, access to advice and role models, supported interaction with professionals and supervised interaction with others. The YMCA also published a further report called "Out of Service" in early 2020 which supports this evidence, making direct links with the loss of these services as a result of the Austerity policy introduced by the Government, and the rise in knife crime (p.1). The YMCA observation in the foreword to this report argues

"No part of society could be expected to suffer almost a billion pounds worth of real term cuts and for there to be no consequences across our communities." (YMCA, 2020. p.1)

Table 11.1 The collapse of youth services in the UK, 2012-19

	2012/ 13	2013/ 14	2014/ 15	2015/ 16	2016/ 17	2017/ 18	2018/ 19	Total 2012-19
Youth work jobs lost	1,126	864	894	768	431	245	217	**4,544**
Youth centres closed	175	184	126	118	64	65	31	**763**

Source: UNISON, 2019

This table refers to the UK generally, rather than London, but the closure of centres in which young people can meet, exchange views, play together in sports, interact and receive support from trained workers has been a material loss keenly felt by young people and those that work with them. This is evident in the comments reflected by research participants as in R:6 above. In effect, it means that the options for young people to meet in a structured and often caring environment are now very limited. Churches still offer youth provision to some extent, but the scale at which voluntary services have been decimated since 2010 means that volunteers cannot possibly fill the gap and make up the deficit. The above-mentioned YMCA report commented upon the loss of youth centres and makes a further direct link with the rise in knife crime.

> "The day-to-day impact of youth services often goes unnoticed by the public, but the consequences of these cuts cannot be underestimated. Cases of knife crime, mental health difficulties and social isolation among young people continue to rise, while the number of services available to positively intervene and prevent such cases continues to decline." (YMCA, 2020. p.2)

R: 9, a youth worker in central London, said in response to the author's questions about what is needed for young people now, argued:

> "It's money and resources. I still find it hard to accept that the government can't see it's worth investing in our children: not just middle-class kids with a support network and family, but all kids, whatever their background. We need resources to help look after these children, and that's what they are: children........ Anyway, these are not kids who just whine about being abandoned, they really are alone, and there's only one of me in this patch." (R:9. 18 August, 2018)

adding a final sentence on the extent of the cuts to youth provision in London, leaving him as the only remaining detached youth worker in the area.

To expand on the loss of public support services, and youth services in particular: local councils in England have borne the brunt of the cuts to the public sector (Roberts, 2019). These Authorities are the providers of Youth Offending Teams, Community Safety, social and caring services which includes social workers, community development teams, hate crime workers, youth workers, public health support and professionals. The cuts have seriously affected local councils' ability to discharge their statutory obligations, and this includes supporting vulnerable young people, some of whom are heavily involved in the knife crime issue.

Chapter 12

Cuts to services and local authorities
in Britain

Focusing on the loss of public sector funding may not seem an obvious place to undertake research into knife crime. It is, however, absolutely central to any suggested remedies for the violence. It is through local authorities that funding for community safety is funnelled. It is here that the links with communities and young people in a given area are made, and such links are made through PCSOs, local authorities, education and community organisations and public health, most of whom work closely with social services, council- based children's services, Probation, Police and Housing. Local councils are crucial in providing services for young people in Britain, but these services must be properly funded. It will be remembered that in the introduction to the book, the author described the devastating experience of having to let a community down having gained their trust when funding for the community service was cut. Sustained, well-supported funding is essential to the restoration of services.

In 2018, the Comptroller and Auditor General published a report on the financial sustainability of local councils in Britain, reporting on a near 50% loss of government funding for the provision of public services (p.4) whilst highlighting the danger to the future provision of basic services such as Adult Social Care and Children's Services (Comptroller and Auditor General, 2018. p.11). The Children's Society reported on this, registering their concerns about the possible "harm" to children as a result of government cuts to local authorities (2019). They highlighted a particular anxiety relating to those children who are most vulnerable in society, where cuts are more likely to be felt. Not least among these are those with mental health issues, as highlighted in the YMCA report quoted above (YMCA, 2020).

In April 2019, the House of Commons Committee for Housing, Communities and Local Government issued their report on the cuts and children's services stating that

"We heard about a system at breaking point, increasingly reliant on the goodwill of social care professionals; the children supported by or in the care of councils are some of the most vulnerable in society and deserve

better." (HM Government, 2019. House of Commons Committee for
Housing, Communities and Local Government, p.3 (b)).

This is not a comment from an outside body levelling criticism at the
Government, but it is the Government's own House of Commons Committee.
It should be remembered at this point that services for children would include
providing support and contact for so-called "vulnerable" children in local
areas, towns and cities across Britain. Within this bracket are those children
who suffer neglect, domestic abuse, poverty and deprivation: the very children
and young people most at risk of becoming involved in knife crime through
various routes. But the removal of funding for local authorities would not only
include children's services. Cuts to the public sector means that all public
services provided by local authorities will be affected such as social services,
community safety, public health, housing, benefits and youth services. It also
includes the police and other nationally provided public sector services.

The policy of removing funding from the public sector was instigated by the
Coalition Government which came to power in Britain during 2010. Austerity
was a conscious policy decision applied by the Government at the time under
the banner of reducing the UK monetary deficit. Theories about Austerity's
ideological roots, its moral foundation and the intentions behind it are many
(Hayes, 2017; Lazzarato, 2012; Lord, 2019; Panton and Walters, 2018).
Irrespective of the background to Austerity, the effects have been devastating
for public services in Britain. For example, Hayes (2017) argued that Austerity
is not just "a fiscal debt reduction strategy" (p.22) but it appears to be much
more a means of transferring a financial deficit from one section of society to
another. He suggests that this debt is transferred not just from the private sector
to the public, but from the rich to the poor. He further argues that this has been
conducted against the most socially and economically vulnerable members of
society, which in his view has been both a disproportionate and deliberately
targeted (2017, p.23) process. Here, responsibility for the 2008 global financial
crash (Hayes 2017, p.23; Roberts, 2016) has been effectively reallocated from
the private to the public sector.

Panton and Walters' 2018 article advances the view that the policy of Austerity
was an essentially ideological act but they set out the case for a different view
around the intention that lay behind it. When discussing regeneration schemes
in local authorities, they identify Government measures such as the
establishment of Local Enterprise Partnerships (LEPs) in 2011 and the reduced
capacity for local authority borrowing as the means by which the private sector
can become more engaged in regeneration (2018, p.164). The article discusses
what Panton and Walters (2018) describe as the ideological nature of this move
on the part of the UK Government, arguing that this follows a marked trend

towards neo-liberal economics in which the private sector is the dominant actor in the provision of public sector services. According to Deas and Doyle (2013, p.377) this affects local government and urban regeneration because as state involvement recedes, the need and desire for urban regeneration increasingly lies with private-sector funders.

With regard to knife crime, what must concern us here is the gradual contraction of the public sector by the Coalition and Conservative governments since 2010 through a series of policy decisions related to the notion of Austerity. Since this time, a succession of Austerity-related policy changes have negatively impacted the provision of public services at local level (UNISON 2018 (a and b); Buck, 2018; Emerson, 2017; Panton and Walters, 2018; Hastings et al, 2015).

Respondents for this research cited aspects of government policy change over the last 10 years, especially with regard to cuts in local youth services. Those services referred to in the interviews specifically were cuts to youth provision in local areas, cuts to community support workers, community centres, probation, policing, housing and housing staff plus benefits changes.

> "What if the adults and people in authority just abandoned you and left you to yourself in your community? What if the options you thought you had for housing, for benefit and for meeting up with your mates have all gone? You're going to think you're on your own. People who feel vulnerable often turn to aggression – especially kids. That's what we are seeing now isn't it." (R:12. 19 July, 2019)

These concerns have been echoed in the LGiU's State of Local Government Finance Survey (LGiU, 2018). Cuts to public spending were and are part of the overall Coalition, then the Conservative policy of Austerity following the financial crash of 2008 (Roberts, 2018). The Local Government Association highlighted their concerns in 2014 where they warned that statutory services could not be maintained in the face of large-scale cuts to public services (LGA, 2014).

Local networks at every level have been adversely affected by these cuts. This first became more obvious during the author's research in London during 2018. Moreover, what must be pointed out is that London is not alone in their struggle with local authority cuts. Britain as a nation is at, and in some cases beyond, crisis point in children's services, adult social care, probation, housing, homelessness and many other services (Roberts, 2019). Some local authorities have experienced financial collapse plus swingeing cuts to their "core" offer to local residents (Chakelian, 2018;). In fact, the House of Commons Housing, Communities and Local Government Select Committee says in its report during August 2019 that the Government had been "derelict" in its own duty "to local authorities by failing to set out a funding settlement that addresses immediate service pressures or plan for future challenges" (HM Government, HCLG Select Committee, 2019 (b)). In view of these issues, the focus for this research must be the effect such cuts have had in local areas upon communities, young people and service providers, including the third sector, and the need to restore such services.

Research undertaken by the Lloyds Foundation for the organisation Third Sector (Ricketts, 2016) shows that in addition to cuts made to local government, many charities have lost up to 44% of their funding. Local authorities in Britain are a prime source of funding for charities in villages, towns and cities, but with little to go around for core public services, funding for charities has been cut. This means that the smaller charities are particularly vulnerable, and local young people's support groups and clubs often fall into this category. In practice, therefore, even those few youth clubs offered by churches and the third sector organisations may now be under threat.

Where this has impacted young people, in London and in towns and cities across England, is in removing not only a safe place to go, but the network of support services that goes with it. With nowhere to go, no one to ask for help, and no one looking to offer it, youngsters are going to get the sense that they are abandoned to their fate. There is a perception that the state has "withdrawn" from communities (Teymoori, Bastian and Jetten, 2017) echoing the notion of Anomie described in the first chapter. The insight of one young person interviewed as part of a group helps us see what the solution is:

> Res 5: But some kids don't got no life but social media, right? The youth clubs all shut. We got this one that's left and its like really full innit.
>
> Res4: You don't even know you don't. It's not like youth clubs and stuff, it's everything. It's everything we've lost innit. (R:6. 13 July, 2018)

These children (aged between 11 and 15) were interviewed as a group and have an intense feeling of loss over the closing of local services ("everything we've lost"). The reinstatement of the infrastructure that supports children in communities is therefore essential to tackling knife crime. As one Police Community Support worker put it.

> "We see what's happening in communities right at neighbourhood level, right at house level sometimes and I'm really not surprised that all this is going on. What do you expect when you take stuff away from communities and from the kids?" (R:23. May, 2018).

This view was reflected by a charity worker/former Probation Officer, who mentioned the resentment felt at the closure of local amenities and services.

> There's long standing resentment against the councils and the government for taking away what many of them feel is their safety net. For some, though, it's more of a signal to do what the hell they like. They know the police haven't got the resources any more. They know no-one is going to come out to a petty burglary or a scrap behind the bins. The kids just feel they've been left to fend for themselves and it's literally kill or be killed." (R:15. 14 May, 2018).

For the sake of argument, in this instance, let us start from the premise that children's support services were developed to answer a known need in society, particularly among the vulnerable. This is not about party politics, but about responding to the need in communities. There really are those who need support, who need services provided by the state. These services were not developed as vanity projects. Removing them has caused real hardship and distress, both at individual and community levels and re-instating them is now urgent.

Part of the solution to knife crime is to replace local services such as youth workers, youth centres, youth advisory services in schools, youth outreach workers, careers advice, youth pregnancy advisory services and community centres where local people can come together. During conversations about the Cure Violence programme in the USA, R:2 mentioned the traceable rise in gun violence when the funding for CeaseFire and Cure Violence was withdrawn in Chicago (The CeaseFire programme is the local version of Cure Violence). Cure Violence is essentially based upon the central notion that community violence is a public health issue (CVG.org. 2020; Slutkin,2013) and can be contained and reduced in the same way that an epidemic can be addressed. This approach will be explored later in this book, but it must be pointed out that crucially, intervention and support for those involved in the community is absolutely central to the ethos of the programme. The focus here is that where the CeaseFire programme has not been funded locally, community violence rises sharply. This is demonstrated in a diagram from the official Chicago Police Department depicting a sharp rise in the violence after the loss of the funding for CeaseFire workers. These programmes have a visible effect in reducing violent crimes in communities and the loss of support services through Cure Violence is notable here.

**Figure 12.1 The Chicago Killing Epidemic Mar. 2015 began
when Cure Violence was cut**

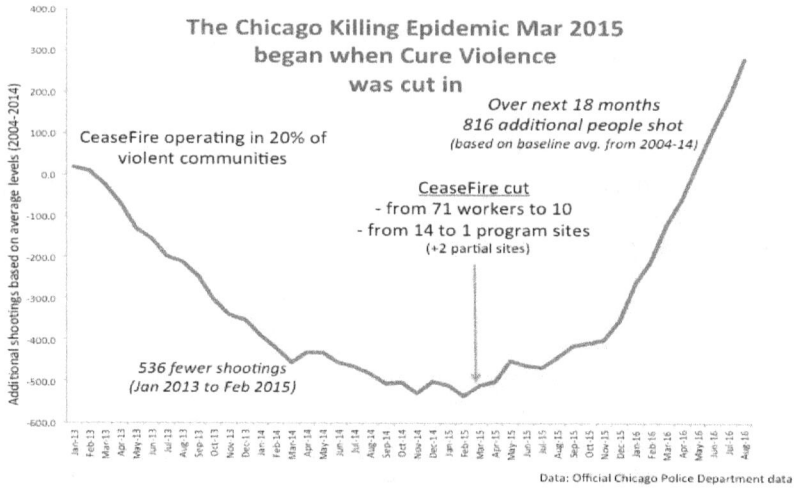

The Chicago Killing Epidemic Mar 2015
began when Cure Violence
was cut in

Over next 18 months
816 additional people shot
(based on baseline avg. from 2004-14)

CeaseFire operating in 20% of
violent communities

CeaseFire cut
- from 71 workers to 10
- from 14 to 1 program sites
(+2 partial sites)

536 fewer shootings
(Jan 2013 to Feb 2015)

Additional shootings based on average levels (2004-2014)

Data: Official Chicago Police Department data

Source: Official Chicago Police Department data

Funding and support are crucial for the success of such locally-focused programmes both in the USA and in the UK. It is also noteworthy that during the research in Glasgow for this book, agencies were keen to point out that they are supported and funded either by central government or other means. The outcome in Scotland, therefore, is a funded and supported network of partnerships and collaborative working that help the VRU to achieve their goals in reducing knife crime and violence. Youth services, and other community services, must be properly co-ordinated and run with support from local authorities: relying on ad-hoc arrangements by ad-hoc funded local charities will not be sufficient to address the issue. The author asked a Chief Inspector in Glasgow where he would cut money if he had to. This officer said that he would look at the estate first, then supplies. At no point in the discussion did he say that front line services, community partnerships, PCSOs or youth services would be cut (R:19. 3 September, 2019).

SR: "If I were a politician, and I asked you to find savings of many millions, where would you make the first cut"

CI: "Good question. I would look at estate, co-location, then maybe suppliers"

In Britain, the very first cuts to public services were Youth Services and Libraries, as the Revenue Support Grant (RSG) to local authorities was cut

(Parliament UK, 2011). The RSG literally provides central government grants and funding to local authorities to support the provision of services. The RSG is part of the funding picture in England, not the whole. Other funds derive from the Business Rates and council tax revenue (Institute for Government, 2020). The following graph from the Institute for Government in Britain shows the rate of decline in central government funding for what they call 'neighbourhood' services up to 2018. These neighbourhood services include those mentioned above that directly support young people in communities.

Figure 12.2 Local authority spending on Neighbourhood services has fallen by 28.1% since 2009/10

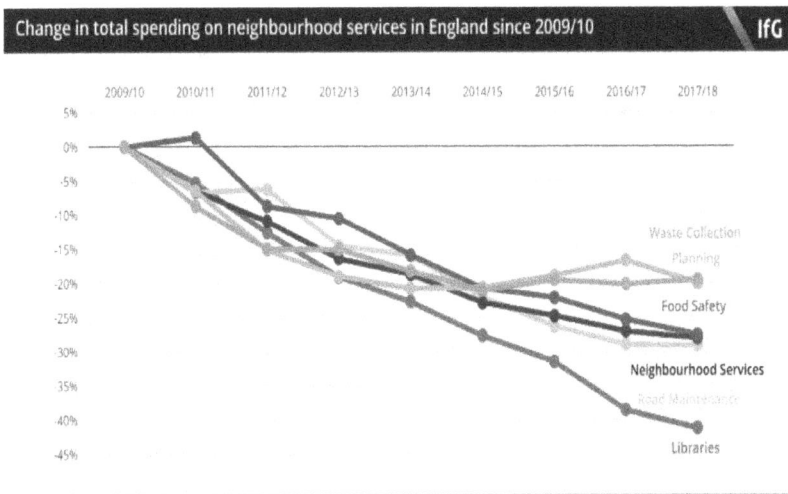

Change in total spending on neighbourhood services in England since 2009/10   IfG

Source: Institute for Government analysis of Ministry of Housing, Communities and Local Government, 'Revenue Expenditure and Financing England', RO2 and RO5.

Source:
http://twitter.com/intent/tweet?text=Local%20authority%20spending%20on%20neigh bourhood%20services%20has%20fallen%20by%2028.1%25%20since%202009%2F10

In terms of neighbourhoods, strong community networks and partnership working is effective where those partnerships and networks are strong (Roberts, 2016). The derivation of that strength often comes from high trust between partners and a history of reliable or trust*worthy* behaviour (Fukuyama, 1996). Local services with strong statutory support can be very effective in bringing about more cohesive local communities. Take these things away and increased violence can ensue as shown above in the withdrawal of the Cure Violence funding in the USA. None of this will come as a surprise to those working in the services or to those using them. It is common sense to respond to the demonstrable neediness of society at all levels, and it is a statutory duty for local councils, especially where there are proven vulnerabilities in communities.

Support for vulnerable people is a complicated issue, especially in modern society. Community support has changed over many years and for our young people and those involved in knife crime, this is a significant issue. Young peoples' feelings of abandonment and aloneness are features that emerged over again within the interviews for this book. At this point it is worth considering the community environment in which our young people live their lives in modern Britain and the role it may have in youth violence, especially in view of our consideration of Anomie.

Chapter 13

A sense of community

There is undoubtedly a clear role for youth support services in the form of clubs and meeting places, however they are supported, so that young people have somewhere to go and someone to talk to if they are in trouble or are just lonely. However, there is a much wider issue to address in terms of the local sense of community. It is necessary to pause and reflect on what we mean here by the sense of community and the existence of community connections.

Margaret Thatcher's famous, or some would say infamous, comment about there being "no such thing as society" bears further analysis here. What Thatcher referred to in her 1987 comments for an interview given to Woman's Own magazine was more nuanced. She was drawing attention to what she saw as a "sense of entitlement" that she felt people had developed towards the government. Her argument was that government should be there to help those in need as a last resort, not as a first response. She went on to say that problems should not be cast upon "society" to resolve. In that sense, she argued, there is no such thing as "society." There are many who would argue the contrary. Thatcher went on to say that individuals should work together to resolve issues themselves first. The comment "there is no such thing as society" was grist to the mill for her opponents who took it and related it to her policies of neoliberalism and market dominance, seemingly at the expense of ordinary people.

> "telling people that in order to maximise economic efficiency, it was necessary to destroy many of the social ties that kept people in interdependency." (McSmith, 2011)

To reflect further on this comment: McSmith (2011) directly refers to the social ties of interdependency. It is this rather than the interpretation of Thatcher's comments that should concern us here. The social ties of interdependency have indeed been eroded, but we must ask ourselves whether the causes should be solely laid at the feet of neoliberalist policy, as above, or whether there are other causes too?

Social capital and communities

Interdependency, social networks and interconnectedness are words that can be associated with our notion of community, which can be further defined as people in a particular area who are considered to be a unit due to

> "common interests, social group or nationality." (Cambridge dictionary, 2019)

If networks are conceptualised as a group of interconnected people, we can begin to form an idea of how common interests, nationality and social groups bring people together. It is this that we could focus on here and what is now meant by the erosion of such societal networks. It is an issue that has been discussed at considerable length, notably by Putnam in his book "Bowling Alone" (Putnam, 2000). Putnam refers to something he calls "social capital" which strongly reflects our notion of societal networks described above. 'Social capital', is not a term invented by Putnam. Rather, it appears to have been first coined by Hanifan in his 1916 article, *The rural school community center*. Here Hanifan describes social capital as "goodwill, fellowship, mutual sympathy social intercourse among a group of individuals and families who make up a social unit." The notion has a long history that reflects social cohesion and connectedness, but later, Putnam (2000) takes up the idea and explains the concept, referring to social capital as "connections among individuals – social networks and the norms of reciprocity and trustworthiness that arise from them" (p.19). He goes on to describe the positive social consequences of these connections as "mutual support, co-operation, trust, institutional effectiveness" (p.22).

One respondent in the research for this book commented on the effect of the loss of social capital among the communities and youngsters he worked with, arguing:

> People just don't have anything to do with each other now, do they. People don't know their neighbours, kids spend ages in their rooms alone, they have online, virtual groups of friends. Not real ones that they meet up with. They live their lives virtually, not really. The idea of my kids putting down their phones for a single day is really frightening for them. They worry about "missing out" and being excluded from things with their so-called mates. These aren't real connections. They're pretend. They live this life that doesn't give them anything in the real world, and it's that stuff that we've lost. They don't know, and don't want to know, the woman that lives next door, or the guy on the next floor who lives on his own. They don't want to get involved with people any more

and we've lost all those connections: the things that make life a little bit better." (R:12. 19 July, 2019)

Further to these observations, we should also note Putnam's later comment in Bowling Alone (2000) that "schools and neighbourhoods don't work so well when community bonds slacken" (p.27). This should be remembered in the context of Anomie, as discussed earlier. The bonds and connections in society, the regulatory forces, the engagement with civic life are missing in an Anomic society.

Putnam goes further and argues that our economy, democracy and our health depend upon social capital. These arguments were reflected in one of the respondents' comments for this research. In talking about the drivers for the violence that we are witnessing in our communities, R: 10, (12 November 2018) argued

"This is about the warp and weft of society and at the moment, it's really difficult due to the cuts and austerity."

If we look at this quite literally, R:10 seems to be referring to something that another respondent to this research named "the fabric of society" (R:12. 19 July, 2019), the connections and links that are formed between friends, groups, neighbours, parents, clubs and societies.

"It's what you and I used to call the "fabric of society".......... Well, it's the sense of family, the sense of belonging, the sense that this place is my place, the people you know, the places you go. People looking out for each other used to be common,........ but this thing [young people's isolation] is new." (R:12. 19 July, 2019)

Teymoori, Bastian and Jetten (2017) refer to what they call the breakdown of social fabric when describing Anomie as a macro-level perception of society, defining social fabric as trust and consensual moral standards (p.1012). These two factors, they contend, provide "strong bonding capital" to enable social networks that strengthen any weaknesses in society. The connectedness of a strong society, one that experiences things together, is an important focus here.

A community worker who spoke to the author for this research spoke about family connections and the sense of community in one of the London boroughs. She argued

"Mostly these [communities] are all about family: you know, family connections, brothers, sons, sisters, uncles. The Caribbean culture is really strong here."

In fact, (R:1) confirmed that the young people he deals with on Staten Island, New York often have a strong sense of connectedness to their family, their mother, parents, cousins or siblings, but that connectedness can also refer to their gang members (R: 1, 13 July, 2019).

It seems that community bonds such as those described by Putnam above, remain strong among some communities and groups, but less so between modern groups of young people from different areas in London, and perhaps elsewhere too. There appear to be two significant and contemporaneous strata of social capital amongst the young in London today. These relate to the troubled communities which are the subject of this book. The first is that of ethnic communities, the second, that of the gangs. The "bonds" of community, indicated by respondents, are there and significantly, they are present inside individual groups. They are not, however, evident between warring gangs and rival groups of youngsters. This will be discussed later.

How have these community bonds been eroded? Forrest and Kearns' 2001 paper on social cohesion, social capital and the neighbourhood state that the neighbourhood has

"re-emerged as an important setting for many of the processes which supposedly shape social identity and life-chances." (p.2125)

This is an important statement, referring to the place or location where people live as a fertile site for creating the bonds that form the setting for a sense of social identity, which then becomes the background for life chances. They go on to define what they mean by the "ties of community —shared space, close kinship links, shared religious and moral values." Forrest and Kearns (2001) describe the erosion of those ties through a new manifestation of "anonymity, individualism and competition" (p.2125). The cohesive nature of communities has been dislocated through such individualist behaviour and pursuits (Teymoori, Bastian and Jetten, 2017. p.1014). Society in many countries seems to have become more individualistic, promoting an image of the individual as self-determining, autonomous and set apart from others. Conversely, social connectedness is defined as a view of the self "as overlapping with close others, such that one's thoughts, feelings, and behaviours [being] embedded in social contexts" (Santos, Grossman and Varnum, 2017. p. 1228). Although the research by Santos, Grossman and Varnum (2017) relates to a study that included 78 countries rather than just the UK, we can recognise the echoes of their definition of individualism in the comments and statements of the participants in the research for this book. It certainly appears to be the case that our disassociation with our neighbours and immediate groups is on the rise (Parker, 2015; Fevre, 2016). Fevre (2016) cites the weakening of civil society through the loss of trades union power in the UK, the decline in church membership and the retrenchment of the individual into a world of self for this rise in individualism. The significant issue here is between individualism and inequality. Fevre (2016) argues that the rise of individualism is part of the growing divide between the "haves and have nots", which also links with the findings about inequality and community violence discussed in this book. Similarly, Maclean (2020) draws a significant picture of gangs and the fertile ground from which they emerge, describing low community investment on the part of the state (p.1) and profiling working-class young men with a view to targeting them. Gangs do not emerge without cause. As R: 18 (4 September, 2019) states:

> "No kid wakes up in the morning and thinks, oh yeah, I'll join a gang today."

There are reasons why children and young people join gangs, and this results from a picture similar to that described by Maclean.

> "Young street gangs (YSGs) are primarily located in traditionally working-class communities, and chiefly characterised by recreational violence. Members (predominantly young men) typically congregate on street corners, and project their sense of disadvantage and vulnerability into territorial street violence." (Maclean, 2020 p.1)

Furthermore, Maclean (2020. p.6) makes a direct link between violence among gangs, social disintegration and despair when he describes "cracks in the social fabric." These have occurred as a result of the Government policy of Austerity in England and his description closely mirrors the Anomie, or loss of social integration, discussed earlier in this book (Durkheim, 2013). The debate about the rise of violent gangs and knife crime is continued later in this book.

Chapter 14

Communities

Looking back, the discourse relating to social and community cohesion was very strong in the early 2000s when government reports and imperatives tasked local authorities in the UK with actions for integration among ethnic minorities and the loss of social capital (House of Commons Office of the Deputy Prime Minister (ODPM), 2004). Social cohesion refers to the bonds between people in a given locality and their shared values. It broke down in a serious way during the early 2000s.

Violent community disturbances in Oldham, Bradford and Burnley in 2001 precipitated an immediate response by the ODPM Committee who visited Oldham to discuss the issue of racial tension and social cohesion in the area. Local authorities in Britain were charged with "breaking down the barriers" between communities to re-establish good relations between different racial and local factions (p.7). These disturbances are not the focus of the current discussion, but the crisis in community relations and the breaking of community ties is important. Oldham, Bradford and Burnley were not unusual and further riots and disturbances have been witnessed in subsequent years, many following a similar pattern of racial tension and social cohesion (Birmingham 2005, Tottenham 2011, Forest Gate 2017). People were losing the ability to 'get on' together, in common parlance. More specifically, the connections between people and their shared experiences were being eroded. Tolerance, understanding and basic community communication seemed to have disintegrated. The unusual feature in this phenomenon is that it has not always been expressed overtly in violence. Anger, hate- speech and intolerance are familiar tropes when considering the expression of the lack of cohesion in the online space.

Research around the link between violent language and violent action (Glenburg, 2019) has revealed a link between the language that individuals hear and see and their subsequent actions, but not all individuals respond with real time action. At a Serious Violence Summit organised by Southampton City Council, the author met R:24 (6 February, 2020) who reported a phenomenon which appears to have emerged via social media. Here youngsters put out a verbal alert through various platforms asking for a "hit" to be carried out on another young person in the community. This may relate to some trifling incident such as disrespecting or "dissing" another youth (Maclean, 2020). The result can be a violent attack involving knives.

Vengeance, racism, intolerance and the violent language used in hate speech do not inspire hateful actions for all people. However, many can attest to the existence of so-called internet "Trolls" who perpetuate unrestrained, often hateful language through the internet (Zezulka and Seigfried-Spellar, 2016). This seeming 'freedom' to give vent to violent language could feed the feeling of isolation amongst young people, instilling fear and uncertainty in some, and perhaps commensurate feelings of violence which could equally fuel actions in terms of knife crime. As yet, there does not appear to be any live research into hate speech and knife crime, but it is certainly the case that violent language seen online can inspire violent behaviour. Glenburg's (2019) article notes that evocative language can encourage the brain to "rehearse" the actions describe in the individual's mind. From rehearsing action in the brain, it may be a short step to enactment. This, he states, is "stimulation theory" (Glenburg, 2019). Such language and such actions may therefore encourage intolerance and poor social cohesion in a particular area or neighbourhood, exacerbating existing tensions.

Chapter 15

The Haves and Have Nots

Forrest and Kearns (2001) begin to discuss the association between the phenomenon of the breakdown of social capital and cohesion when they refer to deprivation and poverty, distancing one section of society from another (p.2126). Perhaps this is better explained in what could be described as the widening gap between the 'haves and the have-nots', or the 1% of the population who have more wealth than the rest of the world combined (Hardoon, Fuentes-Nieva and Ayele, 2016) reflecting a growing concern about inequality (Institute for Fiscal Studies, 2019). Here we may have the beginnings of a different perspective: namely that it may not simply be an issue of social cohesion and race but may have some connection with rising poverty and deprivation. Bringing matters more up to date, it is interesting in the light of this insight to review the comments of the UN special rapporteur's report on poverty in Britain in 2018.

> "It thus seems patently unjust and contrary to British values that so many people are living in poverty. This is obvious to anyone who opens their eyes to see the immense growth in foodbanks and the queues waiting outside them, the people sleeping rough in the streets, the growth of homelessness, the sense of deep despair that leads even the Government to appoint a Minister for suicide prevention and civil society to report in depth on unheard of levels of loneliness and isolation." (Alston, 2018 p.1)

Evidence from participants in the research for this book highlight the significance of the issue of poverty and deprivation in social cohesion and the devastating effect on children.

> "I can take you down the foodbank right now and show you young children who only want something nice to eat. They don't ask for phones, or iPads or any of that stuff. They just want decent food and a place to feel safe. They don't have that in this part of London." (R:8. 20 June, 2018)

Or the former probation officer who spoke to the author in 2018

> "These are kids that no one wants, sometimes not even their own mums. They are out on their own some of them, and they ruin it for all the kids. Don't forget though, these kids have been abandoned by us since the cuts. They're left to themselves in homes where there is usually one parent struggling to cope with overcrowded accommodation and deprivation." (R:15. 14 May, 2018)

This is an environment in which children, and their parents are unable to manage and deal with everyday existence in towns and cities where deprivation, inequality and poverty are rife (Ofsted 2019, p.5). They struggle with an environment of fear and suspicion, of rivalry between gangs, of grinding scarcity in which children just want a roof over their heads and enough to eat. British society now sees children as young as 9 possessing knives from a sense of fear in their communities, (The Independent, 2018 (c)); Child poverty in London is at the highest rate for any English region in 2019, (Child Poverty Action Group, 2019); 27% of Londoners are in poverty, (TrustforLondon.org, 2017) and 14.3 million people in Britain are in poverty, (Social Metrics Commission, 2019, p.5).

The link between poverty, inequality and the loss of social capital begins to become clearer in light of this evidence. Where people are struggling to find enough money to feed themselves, enough to heat their homes and enough to survive from day to day, it may not be difficult to see what has happened to social cohesion. As argued by Agnew, (1992):

> "people engage in crime because they experience strains or stressors. For example, they are in desperate need of money, or they believe they are being mistreated by family members, teachers, peers, employers or others" (p.2).

General Strain Theory argues that serious crime can be found in communities where such strains as poverty, deprivation and hopelessness are experienced at their most intense level. It also embraces the notion of the way that the social environment, or context, affects crime (p.20). Anomie in society, the feeling that all restraint and regulation have collapsed, that literally 'no one cares', provides a social environment in which those experiencing strains can, and do, respond with violence. Teymoori, Bastian and Jetten (2017) describe the anomic society in which moral standards have disappeared, generalised trust is missing (including trust in government), and there is a feeling of fear (p.1011). This, they note, can be most poignantly experienced in groups with lower socio-economic status. The links with such strains as poverty, deprivation and hopelessness cannot be ignored. It is possible here to make the association between Hermeneutic Phenomenology and the connections between individuals' shared experiences. Those under such strains appear to share the experience in groups that access state services through benefits, social services, housing and foodbanks. The clear message here is that those experiencing strain in local areas are often known to each other; poverty happens, as Merton (1938) argues, to those in low socio-economic groups and such groups tend to be housed together in locations in which the state provides housing, or not if you are homeless like some of the youngsters who took part in this research. It must not be assumed, however, that there is little positive social interaction in these circumstances. Far from it. Many of the communities whose young people engaged in this research were loving and strong with family groups strenuously supporting their loved ones. In others, however, the social fabric was threadbare, to say the least, and in these areas, poverty, neglect, violence and homelessness were rife.

Social capital and community connectedness are no longer regularly supported by our public services due to the loss of funding from central Government in the form of the Revenue Support Grant. PCSOs, neighbourhood policing, social workers, youth workers and other community professionals (Roberts, 2019) have been withdrawn as a direct result of cuts in public services spending by the Government. Moreover, the effects of deprivation fuel the temptation for youngsters to get involved in organised crime. As one respondent for this research involved in so-called County Lines argued:

> "My mum, she knows. I can pay her what she needs from robbin' and stuff and she don't ask no questions. She knows like. I ain't never going to be able to afford no nice place like, you understand what I'm saying."
> (R:14. 12 June, 2018)

This young man felt he had been forced into County Lines through his personal circumstances. He lived in an overcrowded council flat with his mother and several brothers. He wanted to do his best for his mother and felt that the only way to support her was through dealing drugs. An intuitive interpretation of the term "County Lines" could evoke the notion of county boundaries for the lay person, but this network of drug-dealing specifically targets the shire communities, towns and villages in Britain beyond the major conurbations. Where dealers have saturated the drugs market in the big cities, further markets are accessed within the rural and county areas in smaller towns and remoter areas (Robinson, Mclean and Densley, 2019. p.694; Whittaker, Cheston, Tyrell, Higgins, Felix-Baptiste and Harvard, 2018. p.5, p.11). Young, and sometimes very young people are used as "runners" taking the drugs to rural communities whilst the "line" refers to the phone line used for communication between the dealers and runners. Hence, "County Lines" (Roberts, 2019). For a further exploration of this issue, see page 80 of this book.

Chapter 16

Neighbourhood Policing

Social capital and community connectedness are also strongly supported by effective and regular neighbourhood policing. This has, however, been a high-profile casualty of the cuts to policing in England. There are those that directly connect social capital with social order, the latter being a product of the former (Somerville, 2009. p.2), meaning that with robust and functioning social capital, social order can follow. The policing of that social order, Somerville (2009) argues, is achieved not merely through the presence of a police service, but in the community utilising individuals and organisations (p.2) in the context of family, community, market or state. This description of a local area or neighbourhood refers to a healthy, high functioning and high trust environment. Since the lack of community cohesion in Britain has reached such worrying proportions, (Walton and Falkner, 2019) it would be logical to examine the effects of the policy decisions which have eroded neighbourhood policing in recent years.

Neighbourhood policing refers to the police working in partnership with communities. The College of Policing refers to it in the following terms:

- Police officer, staff and volunteers accessible to, responsible for and accountable to communities

- Community engagement that builds trust and develops a sophisticated understanding of community needs

- Collaborative problem-solving with communities supported by integrated working with private, public and voluntary sectors.

(College of Policing, 2019)

The efficacies of neighbourhood policing are well documented by the College of Policing (2019) referring to "targeted foot patrol, community problem-solving, ... a focus on delivery [to] address known problems." The purpose is to become aware of, and to be in touch with local areas, deploying named police personnel to communities where local people can become familiar with their local police. Tapping into local networks where intelligence can be gleaned about local trouble spots and potential flashpoints is crucial for maintaining social order. A Police Community Support Officer interviewed in 2018 argued:

"We know the communities, we walk them, we know the people in the local area and we know who does what. We know the homeless guys, we know the problem kids, we know the problem areas. That kind of intel' is vital. It's how we help the warranted officers – giving them all that intelligence so when a crime is committed, we will probably know who did it and where they go." (R: 16. 22 April, 2018)

Neighbourhood policing was developed in the first ten years of the 21st Century, (Higgins, 2018. p.7). In 2004, the Government White Paper, "Building Communities: Beating Crime" (Home Office, 2004) advanced a commitment to the national rollout of Neighbourhood Policing. Underpinning this commitment was a £50 Million fund (p.7) and 25,000 Police Community Support Officers (PCSOs) to provide "a constructive and lasting engagement with members of [the] community" (p.7). The intention was clearly to build closer relationships and more responsive relationships with local communities. It is not difficult to see why. Crime is undertaken in local areas by members of communities. It is not planned openly, on a national platform so that everyone else is aware. On the contrary, intentional criminal activity is covert in the planning, if more visible in the execution. It therefore seems reasonable to conclude that intelligence about such activity may be more accessible to local PCSOs who know their communities well. Neighbourhood policing was put forward as a response by the Labour government to what was considered a completely transformed environment in which the police operated (Home Office, 2004. p.6). Areas of concern were set out as rising expectations on the part of the public, the influence of technology and the rapidly changing types of crime were witnessed.

When the Conservative/Coalition Government took office, the Home Secretary at the time, Theresa May, oversaw widespread reforms to policing, including the election of Police and Crime Commissioners (Higgins, 2018 p.12) under the terms of the Police Reform and Social Responsibility Act (HM Government, 2012). Over time, decision-making about local policing devolved to Police and Crime Commissioners and the funding available for local and neighbourhood policing was not ring-fenced, gradually becoming one with the Police Main Grant (HMIC, 2013; Loveday and Roberts, 2019). It was from this fund that money for PCSOs and neighbourhood policing derived. Policy decisions such as this have resulted in a retracting of neighbourhood policing and the ethos that went with it. The comments of five former Commissioners of Police for the Metropolis in the Times newspaper draw attention to the disastrous consequences of the reduction in neighbourhood policing, which Sir Mark Rowley regrets in the Policy Exchange report "Rekindling British Policing" (Walton and Falkner, 2019).

"The police service..........has had its resources drained to dangerously low levels. The reduction of police and support staff by more than 30,000, the virtual destruction of neighbourhood policing, and the inadvisable undermining of police powers such as stop and search, have taken their toll" (p.2).

Neighbourhood policing and its decline have been highlighted by Sir Mark Rowley in the above report as an urgent challenge for current Prime Minister, Boris Johnson. He argues:

"The operational challenge presented by a widening mission is now threefold........to tackle the rise of knife crime and other violence, often driven by drugs gangs and other organised crime networks whilst re-establishing community policing to address local concerns..." (p.1).

Community and neighbourhood policing establishes vital links with local intelligence, heightens police responsiveness, supports the development of trust between local people and the police and enables the more rapid detection of crime. It is small wonder, therefore, that the disintegration of neighbourhood policing is a key challenge highlighted by Walton and Falkner (2019) in which they argue that "visible neighbourhood teams have shrunk or been disbanded, giving the impression that the police have given up the streets to gangs, thieves and drug dealers" (p.4). A former gang member interviewed in 2018 argued that he need not concern himself with the police because they no longer respond to crime in his area.

"Why should I worry about them? They don't worry me no more." (R:14. 12 June, 2018)

As this section of the research is dedicated to re-establishing links with communities, it is clear that the reinvigorating of community and neighbourhood policing (for which there is strong evidence to show that community-based police personnel reduce crime and disorder) is a key strand, alongside that of the loss of social capital in our society. We must give our full attention to our communities and the best way to repair them after the fractures and dislocations of the last ten years. The fabric of society is now threadbare and the musculature of the policing body has been compromised – but it is hoped, not irrevocably.

Chapter 17

Gangs

There are strong connections with the issues of neighbourhood policing, social cohesion and gangs in localities. R: 17 (21 August, 2019) discussed the links between neighbourhood policing and gangs when he argued:

> "Of course they're related. If you know your community, as in neighbourhood policing, you know your local gangs. That's the connection. Without that intelligence you lose the crucial link to the local problems in a given area." (R:17. 21 August, 2019)

Problems with gangs and gang-related violence is an issue we are witnessing in the high-profile media coverage of inter-gang warfare in our major cities, especially in London (Kirchmaier and Villa Llera, 2018. P.10). It is an escalating problem, as is the complex question of why young people should be joining them. Kirchmaier and Villa Llera (2018) found that children under the age of 15 were a consistent feature of the data on gang membership throughout their statistical sample. Very young people are clearly members of these gangs throughout London, with 44% of wards in the city demonstrating gang membership (p.10). It appears to be young children who participate, young children who are members of gangs in London. If we consider this, a question may arise: why are very young children participating in these gangs? What is it that gang membership gives them?

The connections that indicate the presence of social capital between young people and their communities are much less visible, as discussed. However, we should be aware that close connections, networks and ties familiar to us in the existence of social capital can be quite visible in gangs and seem to denote family-community type connections. It is important to note that these connections are not positive. Although there appears to be a strong sense of mutual identity in gangs, it appears to be very loosely hierarchical, dominated by 'business' in the form of drug dealing and drug running. They are becoming better organised (MacLean, 2020. p.2) for the purpose of their business activities. Yet there are the "connections among individuals – social networks and the norms of reciprocity and trustworthiness" that are similar to the features of social capital that Putnam (2000) referred to (p.19) in the gangs. Unfortunately, the character of these groups or gangs appears to be more a unity that derives from a sense of being 'under siege' rather than one that springs from the desire for a wider sense of community benefit as in Putnam's description.

The National Society for the Prevention of Cruelty to Children (NSPCC) published an article on this subject on their website about the feeling of family in gangs.

> "For lots of young people, being part of a gang makes them feel part of a family so they might not want to leave." (NSPCC, 2019)

Young people at risk, those who feel isolated, those who are vulnerable such as children excluded from school, or those looked after by local authorities are particularly attracted by the notion of belonging to a quasi-family group such as a gang (Children's Commissioner, 2019. p.10). As early as 2008, The Guardian newspaper published an article on the appeal of the family group in gang membership for young people (Davis, 2008). Research undertaken for the Centre for Social Justice commented on this issue in 2009, noting that there is clear evidence that young children substitute the gang for a surrogate 'family'. It is argued:

> "The gang, for a significant number of young people growing up in our most deprived communities, has become a substitute family with the gang leader as the 'father'." (p.27)

This piece of research is significant because the parallels between deprivation, underemployment, poor quality housing and single-parent households is very clear. It is worth noting, therefore, the correlation with the indicators or risk factors that show a propensity to social violence and knife crime within the Government's Serious Violence Strategy (HM Government, 2018. p.38). These closely mirror the social issues highlighted by the Centre for Social Justice research.

i) Postcode gang wars.

When the Coalition Government came to power in 2010, a revision of the existing National Security Strategy (HM Government, 2010) put terrorism and organised crime at the forefront of a range of new priorities. A year later, after the 2011 London riots, the Government set out a new priority to address the "scourge" of youth violence and gangs (Home Office, 2011 p.5). This new focus recognised the serious issue of escalating youth violence in the UK at the time. Central to the fight against gang-related youth violence is the notion of "intelligence led policing." This approach has a long history, but its more modern roots are shown in the 1993 Audit Commission report, "Helping With Enquiries: Tackling Crime Effectively" and Her Majesty's Inspectorate of Constabulary's (HMIC) 1997 report, "Policing With Intelligence." The important focus here is that attention was upon the emerging issues with gang violence in London and elsewhere, and how this was to be addressed. For the purpose of this book, intelligence sometimes collected via young people in gangs themselves, was deemed to be of key importance to the research. For "Policing With Intelligence", local information collected by those involved was to become the focus not just in gang violence but in all types of policing. It is this intelligence which has been shown to be important. Indeed James, (2016, p.24) affirms that much of the value of such intelligence comes from practical experience, and corroboration through those involved is of paramount importance. During the interviews for this study, Police Community Support Officers, (PCSOs) confirmed that such local intelligence is crucial in identifying the locus of criminal and violent activity. PCSOs know their communities and their value in terms of local intelligence has been affirmed many times (Loveday and Smith, 2015; Loveday, 2017), both in scholarly literature and by practitioners (Roberts, 2019). Barnard–Wills & Wells (2012, p.228) support this notion, stating that it would be impossible to gain knowledge about crime without local intelligence. The value of such intelligence, therefore, is not disputed.

There is a clear legacy from the 1990s intelligence-led policing documents with the adoption of the National Intelligence Model (NIM) in the 2002 Police Reform Act (National Centre for Policing Excellence, 2005; James, 2013; James, 2016). The importance of intelligence-led policing must not be underestimated in relation to combating gang violence in the context of this study. It is possible to conclude that intelligence-led policing has suffered as much as other approaches in the aftermath of cuts experienced by all police forces in Britain (Roberts, 2019). This is a concern, given that one of the Key Assets (ICT Police, 2020) in the NIM is "tactical capability", which can include manpower.

With regard to gangs: where groups of youngsters may have grown up together in a given location, it could reasonably be expected that some of these ties would be sustained into young adulthood. Where the opportunity exists, local offenders can band together to form a gang, and possibly develop their activities to become more "substantial organised crime networks" (National Crime Agency, 2014. p.8). The drivers for belonging to a local gang are well documented. As recently as 2009, the Centre for Social Justice, published a report "Dying to Belong" commenting on what it called a sharp rise in gangs and gang culture over the previous decade in Britain (p.20). It should be noted in this report that knife crime and gangs are often conflated, but the two are by no means synonymous (p.21). However, in more recent times, gangs and knife crime have become more visible, especially through the media, and it seems clear that knives and knife crime are indeed a significant element of the gang culture, especially in London and the big cities in Britain (Hesketh and Robinson, 2019).

Notwithstanding this evidence, it should be noted that the conclusions within this report reflect some of the findings from the current study: namely that the drivers for gang membership must be addressed. These are named as

1.   Family breakdown and dysfunction

2.   A lack of positive role models

3.   Educational failure

4.   Mental and emotional health problems

5.   An absence of aspirations

6.   Unemployment and underemployment

7.   Discrimination and stereotyping

8.   Poverty

     (p.215)

With reference to these drivers, some of the risk factors for serious violence named in the Government's Serious Violence Strategy published in 2018, appear to be very similar. Page 35 refers to family issues related to dysfunction, school performance, emotional problems, low aspirations or expectations, and poverty (HM Government, 2018). None of this will be news to those working in the field, but it is striking and noteworthy in the context of knife crime that the background for gang violence and serious youth violence share common features.

The most salient feature of gang and postcode wars is the influence of drugs and drug running. Robinson, McLean and Densley (2019) and Whittaker et.al. (2018) focus on this element of gangs, drawing attention to cities other than London where other areas are designated as hubs for illicit distribution of drugs. These cities are Glasgow, Liverpool, Manchester and other large urban conurbations. The major focus for drug gangs now is upon the 'undeveloped' drugs market in small towns and villages in Britain known as 'County Lines' (Robinson, McLean and Densley, 2019; Whittaker, et. al.; Hesketh and Robinson, 2019; Roberts, 2019). This represents a push by drug dealers operating in the already saturated market in cities to develop new markets in rural towns and villages across the country. The "line" referred to is the dedicated mobile line set up between the dealer and his or her runner. Often these runners are young vulnerable children and young adults. It is certainly true to say that County Lines represents a completely new approach to drug dealing in terms of the exploitation of vulnerable people through violence, sexual violence, coercion, debt bondage and weapons (p.695). Such vulnerable individuals are deployed as either drug runners or their premises used as a base for drug dealing.

Drugs and the buying and selling of them characterise the activities of many gangs in the cities and the influence it exerts over different neighbourhoods should not be underestimated. The ubiquitous nature of the drug market means that gangs are now operating as businesses (Whittaker, et.al. 2018. p.15; Hesketh and Robinson, 2019 p.8) and any encroachment onto business territory or postcode by a rival gang is not tolerated. Such infractions will usually be redressed through violence, often involving bladed weapons. Whatever is done to combat knife crime it must, crucially involve tackling the drugs crisis in England. Such a multifaceted and convoluted problem must surely make us to turn our attention to the question of policy-led solutions and how we can tackle these pressing societal issues through Government action.

The Government's Serious Violence Strategy (HM Government, 2018) is the closest thing we in England have to a comprehensive, updated response to knife crime. It addresses the issue of County Lines, setting out the work of the County Lines Working Group (p.47). This is intended to catalyse cross-party and intergovernmental work on County Lines which should also include other agencies. The magnitude of the problem is acknowledged here and the Strategy recommends partnership and collaborative working by all agencies involved in safeguarding, policing, social care, education, community safety, third sector, local authorities and others. This again is not a new approach and is discussed in this book. The point is that a proportion of young people involved in gangs may seek to fill a need, or variety of needs in their lives. Some of these needs are expressed as the need for belonging, feeling safe or just earning enough money to survive. However, these needs can and should be addressed through social policy remedies. These could include the re-establishment of a robust youth services response from local authorities; re-opening youth centres and youth clubs; youth services that offer counselling and support to those youngsters in need; detached youth workers; properly trained community engagement and outreach workers; support in schools and educational outreach by the police such as that undertaken by Police Scotland and their 'Campus Cops" (R:20. 4 September, 2019; Frondigoun, Smith and McLeod. N.D.) programme; real opportunities when young people leave school, housing options that can be afforded, hope for the future with clear training and educational pathways. The latter must and should be properly supported for those young people who cannot afford to spend time in education or training with the Education Maintenance Allowance (EMA) re-introduced.

ii) Campus Cops

It is pertinent to pause here to review the successful "Campus Cops" programme undertaken in Glasgow by Police Scotland (Gov.Scot., 2010; Glasgow Times, 5th June 2019.). Here, police constables are sited with primary and secondary schools, greeting youngsters as they arrive and seeing them out of schools when they leave. Such officers are sited with the schools, getting to know the children and their teachers. This offers the opportunity for children to get to know the police through the campus cops, eroding the barriers between community and law enforcement. R: 18 (4 September 2019) grew up in Glasgow disdainful and distrustful of the police, fostering an active hatred of them as he grew up. Campus cops help to provide the link between their communities and the law through this daily interaction, and it works (R:26. 3 September 2019). Trust is built up over time, not only with the children in schools but with the parents who see the campus cop every day at the school gate. Relationships are formed and local intelligence is shared. Yet none of this would be so successful were it not for the networked, high trust partnerships at work in Glasgow between the police, local authorities, schools, health and social work. R:20 (3 September 2019) drew a diagram of this interconnectedness for the purpose of this study, showing the ways in which the network functions and overlaps

Figure 17.1 Interconnectedness of services in Glasgow

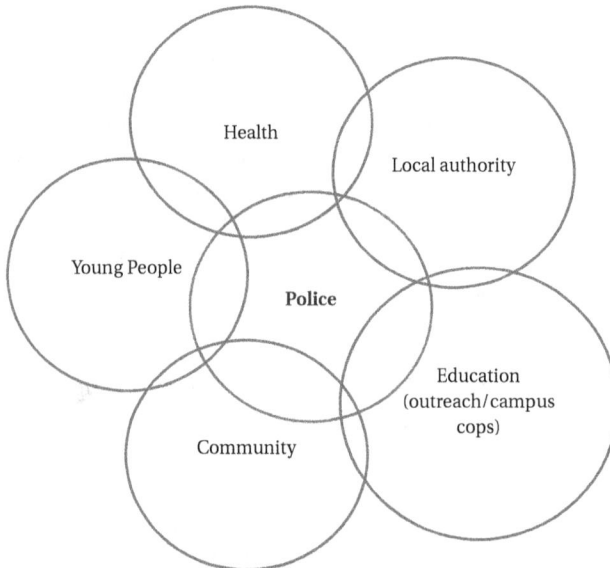

Source: Researcher's own

The purpose of the diagram was to show that in Glasgow, there are strong, overlapping connections between all sections of law enforcement and community actors, as demonstrated during the author's field trip. Partnerships are strong, well established and properly resourced in the city with good, and sometimes very strong, trusting relationships throughout.

However, it should be noted that these suggestions for partnership working and interconnectedness are not luxuries. We can no longer afford to wait for things to get better on their own, as recommended in the Government's Serious Violence Strategy (HM Government, 2018). There will be no new dawn of understanding for children who have been traumatised by knife crime and feel abandoned by the state system. There will be no moment of enlightenment when knife crime will suddenly decline and stop. It must be stopped by those that can stop it, and this refers to those in government at national and local levels; Police, Health, schools, local government, national Government, Housing, charities and volunteers all working together.

Such a call to co-ordinated action has been heard many times before, but it does not appear to have been heeded, even by the same Government that recommended it (HM Government, 2018). Since the project for this book began in 2018, knife crime has continued to rise (Parliament UK, 3 October 2019). There has been no decline. We can speculate that without concerted intervention in the manner described above, the numbers will continue to rise.

iii) Possible remedies for gang violence?

The Centre for Social Justice report (2009) referred to above informed the Government's later policy "Ending Gang and Youth Violence" published in 2011. On page 177 of the report, it is stated that young people felt marginalised and unprotected by a police force that "did not care", echoing the feeling of marginalisation and stereotyping on page 215 of the report and the risk factors in the Serious Violence Strategy published in 2018. These are feelings we have seen before in this book, with youngsters recording feelings of abandonment by the state. Looking across these publications longitudinally, not much appears to have changed over the years in terms of young people feeling and being marginalised in society. Isolation, lack of family support, involvement in youth crime, drugs availability, and the influence of social media may well have exacerbated matters, (Roberts, 2019). At the bottom, we are dealing with the same issues: young people needing support and not getting it: an Anomic society that deteriorates year on year.

However, the variable which does appear to have changed over time is the character of the gangs themselves. Whittaker, et al (2018) undertook some research in Waltham Forest noting that the turf wars between different postcodes were less about the hallowed ground of areas in which gangs operate and are now focused much more on the "marketplace", which clearly relates to drugs as explained above. The Guardian highlighted this research during 2019 noting that the 'outward signs' of gang membership such as gang colours or insignia are now deemed 'bad for business'. Infringement on another postcode area outside your gang's own ground means infringement on someone else's marketplace for drugs (Whittaker, et al (2018). It remains to be seen whether the character of these gangs remains attractive enough for those marginalised youngsters seeking a sense of belonging in today's cities. What may not change is the lure of quick money for young people in deprived communities, living from hand to mouth in streets and communities that feel ignored by government policy.

> "Have you seen inside these estates? They're so overcrowded and the accommodation is like unhealthy. They've got nowhere nice to live and nowhere to feel safe, some of them." (R:8. 20 June, 2018)

ITV news reported on the issue of postcode gang wars in London and the South East during 2018 with a significant quote from the head of the Ben Kinsella Trust, who argued that the violence is

> "just endemic across most of London, particularly inner London. For some reason this isn't just defined to one or two little corners it just seems to have spread and the mindset has crept in across London. It's around social deprivation. If you were to pull out a map which showed the most deprived boroughs I would guarantee there is a postcode war there." (ITV News, 2018).

Here youngsters from different 'postcode' areas wage turf wars against neighbouring or other postcode areas. In some instances, young people are literally afraid of going into another area for fear of being murdered by a rival gang. Sky News published a map of the rival gangs in London (Sky News, 2018) and the widespread influence across the region and one respondent for this research stated that he could not go to another postcode area for fear of being "done"[killed] (R: 9 November 2018). This respondent confirmed that he had been recruited to a gang at the Pupil Referral Unit (PRU) to which he had been sent as a very young boy, and this appears to be a familiar story. A similar story has been reflected by several national newspaper stories in Britain during 2018 and 2019. The Times ran an article on 12 January 2019 (The Times, 2019) which discusses this same phenomenon and the Children's Commissioner said in her report on 27 March 2019 "The gang members know how to find these children and so should we, with the same focus and determination, but this time to help." (Children's Commissioner, 2019). Furthermore, a young offender tragically records his journey through life, growing up in a community without support and attending a school which appears to have failed him. This person was bullied at school from the earliest age and stated in response to a question about when his problems began.

"[at] school. I wasn't diagnosed or nothing but they said I had ADHD and they kept excluding me so I was like sent to a PRU. That's where I got into County Lines man. That's where they get you like, you know?" (R:7. 9 November, 2018)

The author interviewed the same person later in July 2019. This was his story:

SR: Have you gone back to the gang?

R: Yeah.

SR: Why?

R: Oh come on. That's not even a question is it? Why do you think I went back, man?

SR: Was it really difficult to get a job?

R: Sorry, yeah I tried like. But you know what I said last time man. I self-harm, they noticed that at the interview. I got scars on scars man. There ain't no place for me. I just get so twisted up inside I can't even speak no more. I know I'm not worth anything to no one: only my mates [gang]. I make good money now. My mum, she knows but she can't do nothing. When she's in trouble like with money, I can help her now. I ain't gonna see my mum suffer am I?" (R:7. 31 July, 2019)

What seems clear is that once a child has been excluded and sent to a PRU, they are more at risk than if they were in mainstream education (Ofsted, March 2019, p.18). Knife carrying can be encouraged by older adults engaged in criminal activity in order to facilitate an exclusion (p.19) indicating that young children are groomed by these adults for involvement in gangs. It is curious to note that the percentage difference in those carrying a knife within London's PRU's compared with mainstream education is noticeably larger: 47% compared with 25% respectively in the London MOPAC (Mayor's Office for Policing and Crime) Youth Voice Survey 2018 (Ramshaw, Charleton and Dawson, 2018. p.17).

iv) Radicalisation and gangs

During the course of this research, the author noted an apparent similarity between the need to belong to a gang and the sense of family experienced by participants and a suggested sense of family at work in those who have been radicalised. Part of the research for this book took place in 2018. This research included a community event held in Portsmouth during May 2018. This meeting was attended by over 70 representatives of the Community and statutory agencies such as the Police, Community Safety and Public Health. The author asked a group including Police officers, Police Community Support Officers (PCSOs) and charity workers supporting communities the question "Who is it that gets radicalised?." The replies from all participants included "isolation", "poverty", "social exclusion", "lack of support to integrate", "exposure to people with extreme views." In 2012, the Government's Home Affairs Committee published "The Roots of Violent Radicalisation" which on page 8 considers the kinds of people that are vulnerable to radicalisation. The first of these cites "young people and people from lower income and socio-economic groups" (HM Government, 2012. p.8) and although later stating on page 9 that radicalisation can happen to "anybody", youngsters from lower-income and poorer socio-economic groups certainly feature as targets for radicalisation.

Decker and Pyrooz (2012) state that gangs and radicalisation do not necessarily co-relate, but it must be noted that their research is based in the US and did not take into account the latest developments in the UK. In the current climate of violence in London, it seems clear that there are indeed some social similarities in the type of individual that may be attracted to extreme behaviour, either through terrorism or through violent behaviour in gangs. These, Decker and Pyrooz (2012) themselves call "risk factors" (p.153). Isolation and social exclusion are not necessarily "explanatory variables" (p.153) but they do appear to be factors present in the interviews for the research into the London killings in 2018. Hesketh's 2017 article for Liverpool John Moores University in the UK cites his own research into groups and gangs on Merseyside in which he says that the process by which members are recruited to gangs can be seen as a kind of radicalisation (Hesketh, 2017). He goes on to cite such issues as poverty, social inequality, isolation, unemployment, loss of local services and child poverty as factors in the process of attraction to gangs. As noted above, HM Government's Serious Violence Strategy (2018) notes on page 35 that some of the risk factors involved in serious violence are "family socioeconomic situation" and "local deprivation." This view is firmly reflected among the respondents for this research. As the social landscape in cities changes (Rae, et al, 2016), it could be that the "explanatory variables" (Decker and Pyrooz, 2012) are changing and that we are now seeing a stronger correlation between the social conditions and processes used to recruit young people to gangs and the route to radicalisation in communities.

Chapter 18

Deprivation, policy, race

Some changes in government policy are worth noting at this point. In the context of rising poverty, social exclusion, inequality and the increase in social disorder such as the recent increase in knife crime, it is important to be aware of the Government's policy actions in terms of societal issues. One of the most significant of these is the so-called "reform" of the benefits system and the introduction of Universal Credit (UC). Respected social commentators such as the Joseph Rowntree Foundation (JRF) have expressed their support for the ideas behind UC but have warned that its shortcomings risk exacerbating poverty rather than alleviating it (JRF, 2019). They argue in relation to the introduction of UC that:

> "It is not right that 3 million people in poverty are set to see their incomes reduced, the majority also in working families." (JRF, 2019)

The rollout of UC has not gone to plan and has put many people in financial hardship. At the beginning of the reform, UC was introduced alongside a helpline which was run by a private company. Calls from claimants to the line were costing 55p per minute (The Guardian, (a), 2017). Chair of the UK parliament's Commons Work and Pension Committee, Frank Field MP argued "The country will be flabbergasted that people without any money at all should be expected to pay for a call to try and gain some help," (The Guardian, (a), 2017) and after pressure from MPs in parliament, the Government made the line free for callers (The Guardian, (a), 2018). In 2018, the New Statesman published an article by Dave Prentis, former General Secretary of the trades union UNISON, arguing that UC had made matters worse for those in poverty. He claimed that UC was driving poor people into debt (New Statesman, 28th November, 2018). Independent commentators such as those providing food for the poor through Foodbanks argued "Our evidence reveals that for many people the new system is making an already bad situation worse" (Trussell Trust, 2018), noting an unprecedented rise in the use of Foodbanks in the UK. This exponential rise in Foodbank use has been commented upon In April of 2019, the BBC published an article on the sudden increase in Foodbank use commenting that foodbanks were now helping record numbers of people (BBC News, 25 April 2019). The article cites research by the Trussell Trust detailing the demand curve from 2008-9 until 2018-19.

Figure 18.1 Number of emergency food supplies handed out
by Trussell Trust food banks

Number of emergency food supplies handed out by Trussell Trust food banks

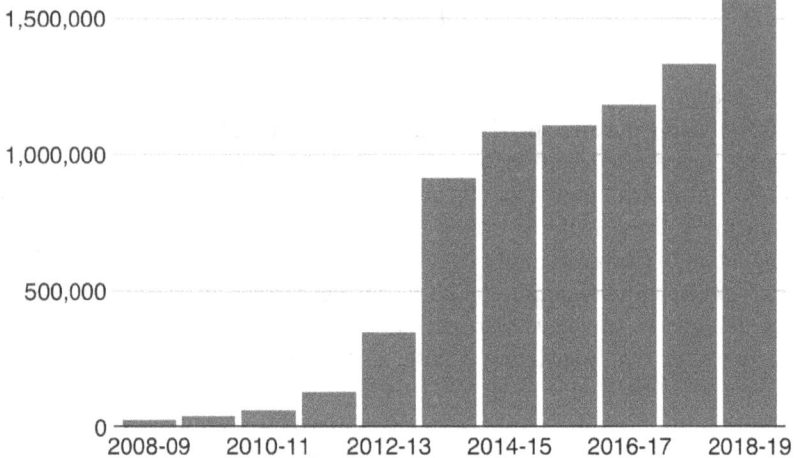

Figure 18.1 Number of emergency food supplies handed out
by Trussell Trust food banks

Source: Trussell Trust   BBC

Poverty is at a record high in the fifth richest country in the world. The United Nations special rapporteur for poverty, Sir Philip Alston, stated after his fact-finding tour of Britain:

> "The bottom line is that much of the glue that has held British society together since the Second World War has been deliberately removed and replaced with a harsh and uncaring ethos." (Alston, 2018)

His comments on the state of poverty in the UK make uncomfortable reading and were immediately refuted by the UK Government (Church Times, 7 June 2019; The Guardian 4 June 2019 (c)). He refers not wholly to UC, but to the policy of Austerity introduced by the Coalition and Conservative governments from 2010. Yet it is worth noting that there is a range of commentators who support the findings of the report (British Medical Journal. 23 May, 2019; JRF, 3 October, 2018; The Independent, 22 May, 2019 (a)).

Spalek in Abbas (2007), discusses "pathways to radicalisation" (p.192) going on to discuss marginalisation and disconnectedness from mainstream society (p.193) citing the disaster of the Iraq war as a feature in the gradual expansion of disconnectedness from others. There seems little doubt that there is a pathway at work through the lives of young people, whether the trigger was the Iraq war or not. Research for this study reveals that there is a racial element to this pathway. So many of the young people who took part in this study were black and one participant who works with young people in central London confirmed the nature of the pathway outlined above, arguing:

> "You mean race don't you. Yes, it's true, so many of them are black or ethnic minority kids. Everyone knows that it's harder for black children to succeed in this country, that's common knowledge isn't it. Well, I see the rough end of that here. They really find it virtually impossible.........
> How can these kids compete when their mum is on reduced benefits, there's no male role model in the family, they can barely afford to eat let alone buy new clothes? I mean, this is reality. What do you expect when these kids leave school having been excluded, sent to a PRU? What have they got to help them succeed? Nothing." (R: 9. 18 August, 2018)

The respondent quoted here refers to the kind of situations she witnessed in her work with communities, and this is a story that appears to be familiar to us anecdotally, and one in which we can begin to decipher a pattern. There are many such stories of deprivation, violence and racial issues, but it is incumbent upon us to review the facts, to establish the veracity of such stories. What exactly could be going on?

Let us examine the comments above in turn. "Everyone knows that it's harder for black children to succeed in this country…" (R:9 above). Rhamie (2007) shows in her book how black, Afro-Caribbean children in UK schools often "have disproportionately high exclusion rates and statements of special educational needs" (p.1). Indeed, the respondent quoted above seems to confirm that this is still the case. It certainly seems to be the case that BAME children do not feel safe at school in London (Ramshaw, Charleton and Dawson, 2018. p.9).

Let us review the evidence for the view that BAME children are being excluded in higher numbers from mainstream education. Is it true that black children are disproportionately excluded from school and have high numbers of special educational needs?

Chapter 19

School Exclusion

In 2005, the Institute of Race Relations'(IRR) reviewed the republication of Bernard Coard's 1971 pamphlet about West Indian children in the UK. This pamphlet talks about perceptions of young black children during the 1960s and 70s and that these youngsters were seen as "educationally subnormal". Portrayed as unable to get to grips with the English language, suffering from negative self-image and struggling with identity crises, many children were written off and subsequently dumped in 'educationally subnormal' (ESN) schools, where pupils were destined to be road cleaners" (Firth, 2005) and not much else. The IRR review continues to question the changing of the perception over time, and notes that by 2004, black boys were three times as likely as white boys to be excluded from school (Firth, 2005). What is more concerning is that 13 years later, in 2018, a research brief was published by Demie which confirms that schools in Britain still appear to be failing young black students (Demie, 2018). He identifies seven key factors which seem to indicate what is happening to young black children in UK schools:

1. Headteachers' poor leadership on equality issues

2. Institutional racism

3. Stereotyping

4. Teachers' low expectations

5. Curriculum barriers and relevance

6. Lack of diversity in the work force

7. Lack of targeted support (pp. 1-2)

He further identifies influential factors which emerged during the study. It is worth listing these in full as these issues have emerged in the study for this research and prior research by the author regarding problems experienced by young black people in British schools and in areas of London affected by deprivation, poor housing and lack of public services.

8. Exclusions issues

9. Lack of parental aspiration and low expectations

10. Low literacy levels and language barriers

11. Absent fathers

12. Single-parent families

13. Socio-economic disadvantage

14. Poor housing

15. Social class issues

16. Lack of role models and peer pressure

17. Negative peer pressure

18. Cultural clashes and behaviour

19. Schools ability grouping and lower-tier entry issues

20. Cultural and identity issues

21. Media negative picture and stereotyping

22. Police stop and search and its negative impact on race issues

23. The pressure of the government's school standards agenda

24. Recruitment and training issues of teachers, Education Psychologists and SENCOs

The immediate question relates to whether these issues are reflected elsewhere in the academic discourse? The link begins to become clearer when searching through the literature. The Social Market Foundation published a press release in 2016 about the growth in educational inequality over the last thirty years. The press release highlighted the issues with educational underachievement in young black children, but crucially, the release makes a connection between deprivation and underachievement in both poor white and afro-Caribbean children. So, it does not seem that educational underachievement is concentrated solely among black children. There is a strong link between deprivation and educational issues for all children. But it does appear to be the case that black children are more likely to be represented in PRU numbers than white children. It is not the intention of this book to look into any accusations of institutional racism, but for those working in this environment, these proportions may not constitute any surprise.

What about the comments relating the Pupil Referral Units? Is this part of the pathway referred to above? Respondent 7 (31 July, 2019) talks about his own route through school, ending in referral to a PRU. He became involved in County Lines drug running almost immediately. Let us be clear, however. Not all children who attend the PRU end up involved in County Lines or in any other form of crime. It is important for our purposes here, however, to note the prevalent discourse. It does seem that the PRUs are an important element of the so-called pathway referred to above.

Although the notion of excluding children from school for a range of issues is not new, the association with a rise in violent crime is. As confirmed by the young black ex offender, R: 7 (9 November, 2018) whose problems began at school, he reports being excluded for undiagnosed ADHD and sent to a Pupil Referral Unit (PRU) where he was recruited to County Lines drug dealing. This is not an unfamiliar pathway to involvement in drugs and criminal activity. It has been featured in several national media outlets, including the Times which ran an article in March 2019. This was entitled The Scandal of Schools For Knife Crime, adding that some PRUs were so bad that are "no more than gang grooming units" (The Times, 3 March 2019). Furthermore, the BBC picked this story up on 8 March in an article entitled "Knife Crime: Are School Exclusions to Blame?" (BBC News. 8 March, 2019) in which it reported that some Police Commissioners had written to the then Prime Minister Theresa May warning that children excluded from school are "sucked into" criminality in these units. The article shows the correlation between school exclusions and knife crime in a table taken from the Department of Education.

Figure 19.1 Number of school exclusions and knife crime offences

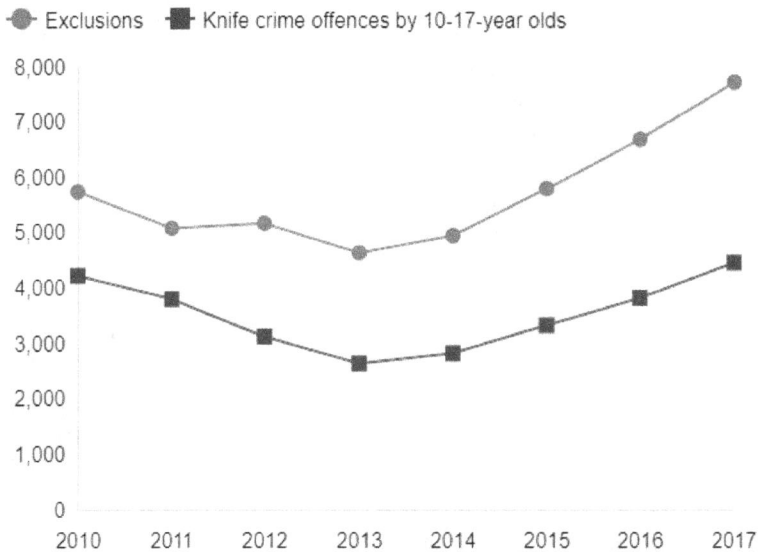

Number of school exclusions and knife crime offences
Permanent school exclusions and knife offences resulting in conviction, England

Source: Department of Education, Home Office

On 28 January 2019, the House of Commons debated this issue under the motion: School Exclusions and Youth Violence (Hansard, 2019). The debate mentions a report from the Ministry of Justice (MoJ) which highlights that 42% of prisoners had been excluded from school with a 63% rise reflecting temporary exclusions. It then goes on to say that exclusion from school can often mean complete social exclusion, particularly if the exclusion is permanent, saying that this leaves children vulnerable to exploitation by criminal gangs. This pattern is reflected in the interviews undertaken for this book, especially among the school-age children. Once a school has removed these youngsters from mainstream education, the stigma and isolation from peers tends to stick. The path from PRU to Prison after exclusion is a painful one to hear.

> "Like from the PRU on, there wasn't nothing for me. Not nowhere. I went from there straight to [gang name] then when I got caught, straight to prison. My probation officer, she told me I'd go back to it. She was right." (R:7. 31 July, 2019)

There does, therefore, seem to be a strong connection, and a clear pathway between school exclusions and youth violence of the type we are discussing here. The social exclusion that can result from school exclusion can mean that youngsters find themselves not only on the edge of school life but on the margins of community life too. If we link this to the notion of social capital (Putnam, 2000), this could very easily mean the loss of local links and connections that could help to re-integrate young people excluded from school. For example: consider the young participant quoted above. After school exclusion, he no longer met with friends from that environment; did not participate in the football team, did not talk to others at school dinners, did not interact with teachers in after school clubs. His mother no longer had connections with the school through parents' evenings or other meetings. Instead, he became an excluded student and excluded member of society with a completely new set of peers, a strange environment that he felt was more like a prison, with daily exposure to other, sometimes very violent and challenging young people. Local youth clubs began to close and he was seen and known in the local area "running" with members of a gang. No one from his school days wanted to know him, including the teachers. School exclusion and social exclusion became more than a reality for him as he participated in the gang and finally went to prison. When the author spoke with his mother, she said "this is a boy let down by the system."

School exclusion resulting in social exclusion is not an issue peculiar to the UK. A rise in both school and social exclusion has been discussed with regard to Australia (Sergeant, 2016) where antisocial behaviour and drug offences appear to be the main reason for exclusion. Sergeant states that exclusion puts children's social development and personal development at risk (2016) referring to studies in the USA and Australia in which it has been shown that school exclusion can lead to an increase in anti-social behaviour, rather than a reduction, (Hemphill, et.al. 2013). The USA/Australia research argues that "suspensions [school exclusions] predict a range of student outcomes, including crime, delinquency, and drug use" (2013, p. 187). It is significant that crime, delinquency and drug use are reflected in the many issues that young people excluded from school in Britain report. The extent of school exclusions in the USA has been steadily increasing, (Hemphill et al, 2013) as it has in Australia where Graham, (2018) notes the increase and the long-term negative impact of school suspension on the life chances for vulnerable and disadvantaged children. This is reflected in the primary research for this book where R:1 confirmed that truancy, expulsion or school exclusion are linked to serious youth violence in the USA, stating "sure, this is a problem for us" (R:1. 13 July, 2019). In discussing school exclusion as part of the penal code in USA schools, Hirschfield (2008) confirms troublesome or 'rule breaking' children were often labelled in the same terms as criminals in practice and policy within the USA school system. Hirschfield's (2008) commentary notes that as early as 2008, children in USA schools were often treated as criminals when breaking or flouting rules in school and were dealt with through deploying armed police arrest, dogs and metal detectors. The links to behavioural divergence and deprivation are well made in the paper, where he cites Wacquant (2001) and argues:

> "The divergence pattern most fundamental and worthy of explanation is that criminalization is more prevalent and intense in schools that are heavily populated by disadvantaged urban minorities (Wacquant, 2001)." (p.80)

Although the majority of the paper focuses on the use of criminal justice type responses within USA schools, the point is clear that there is a definite link between deprivation and deviant behaviour which includes weapon-carrying, in schools. There is also a link between deprivation, school exclusion and children of colour (Hirschfield, 2008. p.82; Sethi et al, 2010). School exclusion is one of the punitive measures used, but the range of remedies available to USA schools appear to be much more closely aligned to criminal justice remedies, particularly in deprived areas, than those in the UK. The pathway from school to prison seems clear, however, in both nations where deviant behaviour, or in the UK, 'challenging' behaviour, is presented in schools.

The Institute for Public Policy Research (IPPR) in the UK published an article in 2017 called "Making the Difference: breaking the link between school exclusion and social exclusion" (Gill, Quilter-Pinner and Swift, 2017) which focuses on the issue of social exclusion as a result of school exclusion. With a foreword by Edward Timpson, former minister, page 7 begins with the argument that:

> "Nowhere is Britain's social mobility failure more obvious than in the example of school exclusion in England. Excluded children are the most vulnerable: twice as likely to be in the care of the state, four times more likely to have grown up in poverty, seven times more likely to have a special educational need and 10 times more likely to suffer recognised mental health problems." (Gill, Quilter-Pinner and Swift, 2017)

The link, therefore, between school exclusion and lack of social mobility is well made here, but there is a further issue here: there are notably some groups of children who seem to be much more likely to be excluded from school.

The Timpson Review (HM. Government, 2019 (a)) further looked at the reasons why this should be the case.

> "Children with some types of SEN [Special Educational Needs], boys, those who have been supported by social care or are disadvantaged are all consistently more likely to be excluded from school than those without these characteristics....... Children from other ethnic groups are more likely to experience exclusion, in particular Black Caribbean and Mixed White and Black Caribbean pupils..... and those eligible for free school meals." (pp. 9-10)

The finding around SEN children is interesting, but it is also noteworthy that children who have suffered disadvantage are more likely to be excluded, alongside children from Black Caribbean, Mixed White and Black Caribbean children. A picture appears evident here in that poor, black or mixed-race children seem to be more likely to suffer exclusion, according to the report. So, this is not merely a question of the environment within the PRUs: it is also about the kind of person you are and significantly, the context that surrounds you "...those supported by social care.... Disadvantaged..... Black.....Mixed White and Black.... Those eligible for free school meals." In considering the Timpson Review in tandem with the profile of young offenders and those involved with knife crime, the pathway we have been discussing appears to become clearer. On the face of it, if you are poor and have free school meals, come from an ethnic minority group, especially Black Caribbean or black/white Caribbean, or have clear disadvantages in terms of Special Educational Needs, you are more likely to be excluded. The reasons for this state of affairs in Education is not part of the scope of this research, but the types of children who are excluded most definitely are. It is doubly concerning to note that children with more than one of these characteristics is even more likely to be excluded (p.10).

We must not lose sight of the wider picture here. These are very striking statistics from the Timpson Review (HM. Government, 2019 (e)) and from other sources quoted above, but there is a major issue at play here. What could have happened to society where children who are disadvantaged in multiple ways, children who are black or mixed race, children who are poor apparently carry 'markers' for school exclusion? What has happened to the social cohesion that we were so concerned about during the late 1990s?

There have undoubtedly been changes in a rapidly evolving society, and it would be naïve to expect things to remain static, but these are systemic characteristics that manifest themselves in our system. We should surely begin to ask ourselves searching questions about the nature of a society in which this could happen and continue to happen. Perhaps it is attributable to the loss of social networks or social capital but there are other very considerable contributory factors.

Chapter 20

Poverty

We will consider the role of poverty in this equation a little further. Teachers who took part in a documentary for ITV Channel Four News in 2017 talk about the ratio of child poverty being one in two children. A teacher at Morecombe Bay primary school comments that children cannot learn when they are hungry or deprived. This does not refer to those who are black: rather to all children who are deprived in British communities. (ITV Channel Four News, 2017).

Research undertaken by this author has highlighted similar issues, in which those who took part mentioned bad housing, lack of access to housing, lack of public services and low police numbers as significant factors in their daily lives and communities (Roberts, 2019). Poverty and deprivation are major drivers for knife carrying and knife crime (Mason, 2019). Furthermore, respondents talked about the state of their public services and housing since the Coalition and Conservative policy of Austerity brought about the cuts to public services. A former prison officer interviewed for this research argued:

> "It's not just services, it's the help that goes with them. For me, this is as much about housing as anything else. Housing is a really big issue in London. No one can afford it. At least no one I know. These kids, they've got nothing you know. The government have taken away all their access to subsidised housing, and their benefits. You know, if they are thrown out of home, and they often are, they've got no chance of housing." (R: 11. 4 June, 2018).

Austerity was not simply a policy of fiscal realignment after the financial crisis of 2008. It initiated widespread social changes that meant disadvantage and deprivation to those most vulnerable and at-risk members of our society. Access to education amid this social crisis is still a very significant problem. Children who do not have a supportive home life, sufficient to eat, heating, safety and enough money to provide basic necessities are not going to learn effectively whether or not they are black. This is a crisis that spans the races, but there is no doubt that within that crisis, black and ethnic minority children are suffering disproportionately.

Chapter 21

Youth violence and the loss

of public services

The loss of public services to support such young people is therefore a serious development. On 31 July, 2019, the Home Affairs Committee in parliament published a report (HM Government, 31 July 2019 (a)) on the Government's Serious Violence Strategy (HM Government, 2018), focusing on the loss of public services and the role this plays in the rise of youth violence. The Committee Report heavily criticises the Government's 2018 strategy which it says "lacks focus and leadership" (p.3) and contains no targets, milestones and lacks clear "mechanisms for driving forward activity at local and national level" (p.3). On page 4, the Report identifies what it calls a "perfect storm emerging from cuts to youth services, heavily reduced police budgets, a growing number of children being excluded from school and taken into care, and a failure of statutory agencies to keep young people safe from exploitation and violence" (HM Government, 2019, p.4 (a)). This supports a growing body of research into youth violence in Britain which identifies the loss of public services as a major contributor to an escalation in youth violence (Roberts, 2019; Buck, 2018; Emerson, 2017; Hastings, et.al., 2015). The Serious Violence Strategy (HM. Government, 2018) itself states that some of the reasons for an increase in young people dying through knife attacks could lay with what it calls "an increase in the number of children considered most vulnerable" and those children who are in care, excluded from school and those without a home (p.43). Moreover, the Home Affairs Committee Report (HM Government, 2019 (a)) analyses the Serious Violence Strategy and cites the Strategy's own exploration of risk factors for serious youth violence which include adverse childhood experiences, male gender, ethnic background, deprivation, school exclusion and MP David Lammy's work on the lack of trust between young BAME communities and the police (p.14). It should be remembered that the acknowledgement of such drivers does not equate to action to tackle the issues.

At this point it must be stated that the correlation between weapon carrying in the USA and the UK diverges in that knife crime is not at the same levels in the USA. As in the comments by R:1. (13 July 2019) "this isn't a problem for us", but gun crime most definitely is. It is also worth recording that there is a fundamental difference in the nature of knife crime to that of guns. It should be remembered that knife crime is an 'up close and personal' offence (Reilly, 2019. p.175) in which the perpetrator must engage with the victim in close quarters. Where a knife attack requires physical contact between people it is less so with gun crime, in which perpetrator and victim can be at a physical distance in order to injure, maim or bring about death. Even so, those in the European region have a high rate of knife carrying due to the availability of knives (Sethi, et al, 2010) and suffer commensurately high levels of knife crime.

Furthermore, there is convergence of opinion that youth violence, especially knife crime, is at its worst in areas of high deprivation and economic hardship, is experienced at schools and in communities where there is poverty and high levels of adverse childhood experiences (ACES). Children excluded from school are at higher risk of falling into youth violence and drug-related crimes and there is a racial element to the susceptibility of children to knife crime (Sethi, et al, 2010) which is linked to deprivation, poverty and reduced life chances.

It should be noted that the UK Government's Serious Violence Strategy names categories of young people most vulnerable to influence through violent crime (p.37). This closely resembles those categories shown in the Gill, Quilter – Pinner and Swift (2017) study quoted above. The list of risk factors from the Serious Violence Strategy (HM Government, 2018) for young people becoming involved in serious violence includes Individual, Family, School, Community and Peer Group risks as shown in the table taken from the Strategy below.

Figure 21.1 List of Risk Factors

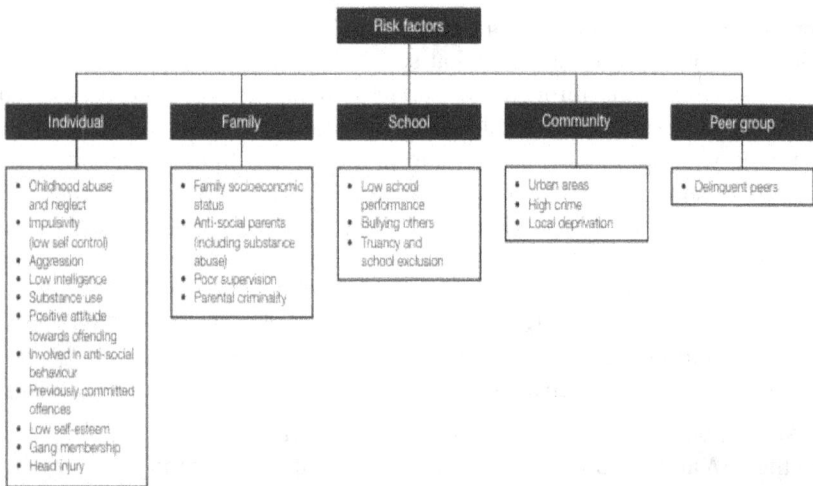

Source: Serious Violence Strategy (HM Government, 2018)

Notice that under Family, low socioeconomic status is quoted as a risk factor, as is bullying, school exclusion and local deprivation under other headings. A child's background that includes such risk factors is well known to those professionals involved in caring for such children, but what is less commonly discussed are the wider effects of strongly punitive, stringent criminal justice remedies for these youngsters when crime is committed. Grimshaw and Ford, (2018) writing for the Centre for Crime and Justice Studies, affirm that "absolute material deprivation has been found to be a factor which determines violence" (p.6), quoting a range of studies connecting inequality with lethal violence. They go on to argue that punitive criminal justice interventions such as stop and search have been shown to be ineffective, quoting Keeling (2017). He stated that stop and search has had a demonstrably negative effect on certain groups and communities, notably the black community. Grimshaw and Ford, (2018) also note the increase in custodial sentencing which they say has been criticised for its ineffectiveness (p.14). R: 1 (13 July 2019) began his response to the author when asked "how can we tackle knife crime?" argued:

> "Show them some love, for gods sake. I'm probably the only one in these kids' lives who has shown them love."

Whilst this is unlikely to happen in our UK schools, PRU's and prisons, it should be remembered that our methods so far could hardly be said to be effective, whether that means more police on the streets, stop and search, referral to PRU's or incarceration in prison. Grimshaw and Ford (2018) argue that policy responses in terms of punitive criminal justice measures seem neither "just not effective" (p.12) quoting a range of research on the questionable effectiveness of custodial sentencing. Perhaps a different approach is required, and it could be one that includes a more humane, caring approach to tackling serious youth violence. This view is supported by recent (Sethi, et al, 2010) and current researchers in the field as well as Grimshaw and Ford (2018) with later research underway by Sanders-McDonagh (2019). Clearly, a supportive and humane approach cannot constitute a stand-alone policy in itself, but perhaps it is time for policy leaders to consider a more holistic view of tackling serious youth violence, including early intervention, youth support and counselling, Violence Interruption, such as that practiced in the USA as part of the Cure Violence programme (R:2. 11 July, 2019), mentoring, the re-establishment of youth services in the UK and better local authority funding to secure a range of support services in the community.

Having considered these issues, there is a further significant element to include. We cannot ignore the rise in young people's involvement in social media and its apparent role in forging connections and networks between them.

Chapter 22

Social media

The author contends that the losses which communities have sustained through the Government policy of Austerity have exacerbated the erosion of societal networks and community interaction, only part of which has been a natural process alongside technological developments such as the rise in social media. The Independent newspaper in the UK ran articles on this phenomenon during 2017 and 18 (The Independent, 2018. (a), (b)). The article reports on research undertaken for the NSPCC in which a 14% rise was reported in feelings of loneliness and isolation; that those who use social media regularly each day feel more isolated. The notion that social media is entirely connective and preserves the sense of community therefore appears fallacious at first glance. The UK Government appears to have reflected these concerns when they commissioned a report on young people's health, social media and screen use in 2018, which reported in January 2019. The report highlights the benefits of social media in connecting young people around the world, but whilst the committee received positive reports, they comment on the unexpected number of reports about the negative effects of young people's engagement with social media (p.5). They highlight the sharp rise in young people's mental health problems (p.7). There is a clear call in the report to improve the evidence base for the proposition that there is a link between a decline in child mental health and social media, but a worrying connection has been made on page 24 of the report in which it is stated that

> "11 to 19 years olds with a "mental disorder" were more likely to use social media every day (87.3%) than those without a disorder (77%) and were also more likely to be on social media for longer" (HM Government House of Commons, 2019 (b))

The report goes on to cite research by the Royal College of Paediatrics and Child Health (p.25) which identifies fairly strong evidence for depression and anxiety in long-term screen use. Evidence for behavioural problems associated with over-consumption of screen time was apparently, weak. However, it seems likely that there is an association with a proportion of young people's negative mental health and social media.

R:1, (13 July, 2019) mentioned a rise in young people's mental health problems when he spoke to the author about his work on Staten Island as a Violence Interrupter. He confirmed that youngsters in his area reported concerns about their mental health, with increases in depression and anxiety that feeds into the violent language used in on social media. He spends two hours each day scanning social media for potential trouble spots or flashpoints, noting the speed of escalation in violent language on social media that leads to killings. The Staten Island programme has reported success in this approach with 900 days elapsing (at the time of writing) since the last young person was killed on the streets. The focus here is the decline in mental health among young people and the rise in social media use and personal isolation. Although social media should connect our young people positively, it often does not and in violent and volatile situations social media can be a vehicle for inciting lethal action on the part of young people, especially in gangs (Storrod and Densley, 2017. p.689). There is no doubt that it plays a role in knife crime and youth violence and there is undoubtedly a pressing need for continued research in this area.

Chapter 23

Framing solutions

It would be helpful to give some focused attention to what such a range of solutions would look like in reality and what our current solutions have achieved. Beginning with some of the suggestions set out above, given that stop and search powers have just been augmented, the evidence so far appears to suggest that stop and search does not work as effectively as we are led to believe.

i) Stop and search

In 2016, the Home Office commissioned research into stop and search initiatives and their effect on violent crime (McCandless, Feist, Allen and Morgan, 2016). Assessing the impact of Operation BLUNT2, (an initiative begun by the Home Office in 2008 to combat knife crime) which showed that whilst the research did not support the idea that stop-and-search reduces crime, it showed that in some localities, there was a reduction in knife crime during operation BLUNT2 (p.3). The Home Office compared the USA and the UK in the research, but eventually found relatively little evidence that stop-and-search has a significant or noteworthy effect on crime reduction (p.11). The effects were considered "marginal" (p.11). This is supported by research published in 2019 by Bradford and Tiratelli, who repeated the conclusion that evidence shows its effects to be "at best, marginal" (p.1). It should be noted, however, that the Home Office report by McCandless et al (2016) states that more research is required into the link between stop-and-search and reductions in crime, especially youth violence. Given that further research is required, it remains a subject of debate as to the efficacy of stop and search and the determination by police to retain it as part of the fight against knife crime in particular.

Stop and Search was originally part of Section 1 of the 1984 Police and Criminal Evidence Act (HM Government, 1984) with its accompanying Code of Practice A which referred to the need for "reasonable suspicion" in stop and search. It was a key change in 1994 that removed the "reasonable suspicion" element of stop and search under section 60 of the Criminal Justice and Public Order Act (HM Government, 1994). Here the police no longer had to have 'reasonable suspicion', but a senior police officer could authorise a stop and search in a given area to prevent serious violence or search for weapons after an event. This was again the focus under section 44 of the Terrorism Act 2000 (HM Government, 2000 (b)) in which the definition of terrorism was widened, effectively giving the police enhanced powers to stop and search anyone without 'reasonable suspicion' (Parmar, 2011). In fact, Parmar (2011) argues that the use of s.44 has resulted in the criminalisation of ethnic minority communities (p.369). In 2011, the European Court of Human Rights ruled that s.44 stop and search was unlawful, violating section 8 of the European Convention on Human Rights (p.371). In the UK, when Theresa May was Home Secretary, s.44 stop and search powers ended in July 2010. Its withdrawal was not universally well-received, especially by senior police officers (Parmar, 2011). However, stop and search persists under s.60 of the Criminal Justice and Public Order Act (HM Government, 1994).

ii) Reasonable suspicion

Currently, any stop and search activity in Britain should include "reasonable suspicion" on the part of the police that the subject is carrying a weapon, or "article" associated with terrorism (HM Government, 2000 (b)). The complexity and controversy around enhanced powers to stop and search has caused some difficulty as 'reasonable suspicion' links very strongly with the notion of the presumption of innocence, which is core to British justice (Picinali, 2014).

 Over subsequent iterations of the Act, reasonable suspicion has been restated and a recent change took place in 2018 when this power was re-established. It was further enhanced in March 2019 with the lifting of two conditions surrounding Section 60 of the Criminal Justice and Public Order Act. The first of these reduced the need for authorisation by a senior police officer and the second lowered the "degree of certainty" (Home Office, 2019 (a)) required by authorising officers. The key change was the word "will" to "may", which referred to the authorising officer's certainty that an incident will take place to one that "may" take place. This enhancement to stop and search powers was intended to relate directly to the acute rise in knife crime. Empirical evidence from this study indicates that many officers consider stop and search a key tool in addressing the issue of knife crime.

 "It has to be part of what we do." (R:19. 3 September 2019)

 Shiner and Delsol (2015) support this view and argue that if stop and search remains part of what we do, it must relate to the way in which we approach crime control and the governance of the nation state (p.31). It should not be seen as a stand-alone tool that has a narrow focus. Perhaps this is the kernel of the issue: that we should be looking at stop and search as it relates to other remedial actions, our governance structures and the ways we have developed our response to tackling youth violence and knife crime. Yet research for this study revealed different approaches taken to the whole notion of stop and search. In Glasgow, police personnel who responded to this research argued that "talk" is the best weapon and first response in stop and search. R: 20 (4 September, 2019) argued that "This is your first weapon [points to mouth] in stop and search. Talk to them first. You know "what's going on lads? How are you doing?" kind of approach." It certainly seems to be the case that there are variations in the use of stop and search among different police forces across the country as shown on page 3 of the Bradford and Tiratelli study quoted above (2019) with the highest use in London by the Metropolitan Police.

Stop and search is not going anywhere for the foreseeable future and continues to be a valued part of the police approach to tackling youth and community violence. It should be reiterated that this is, or should be, a tool among many and given the evidence that it has marginal effects on crime reduction, a review of its use and relation to other remedial actions seems timely.

Chapter 24

Working together to tackle knife crime

In 1998, a new approach to tackling policing and community violence was set out in the 1998 Crime and Disorder Act (HM. Government, 1998; Williams, 2009). Here a plan for local, multi-agency partnerships was set out, establishing Crime and Disorder Reduction Partnerships (CDRPs). These were based in local areas, led by local authorities' Community Safety staff. They were intended to co-ordinate action against crime and disorder in local areas using different agencies such as the police, community safety staff in local authorities, probation, Youth Offending Teams (YOTS), Substance Abuse teams, Social Services, Primary Care Trusts, Fire and Rescue plus other relevant organisations. The approach was hailed as successful (Williams, 2009. p.573) in tackling crime and disorder in communities, and the notion of such a multi-agency approach to local issues was replicated in the introduction of Local Strategic Partnership (LSPs) in the Local Government Act 2000 (HM Government, 2000 (a)). The LSPs were intended as a forum for community action, requiring local authorities to 'lead, but not dominate' (Roberts, 2016) the partnerships in the creation of a Community Strategy for every area in the country. The strategies were intended to articulate a vision for local areas in the long and medium-term, aiming to improve services, amenities, community cohesion and the built environment over time. Multi-agency partnership appears to have been the preferred model for all communities under the Labour government, 1997 – 2010, but the approbation for LSPs was not universal.

Geddes, Davies and Fuller (2007, p.1) undertook a review of the LSPs which was not, on the whole, positive. He argued that the response to the establishment of the LSPs among local authorities had not been one of enthusiasm (Geddes, Davies and Fuller 2007. p.2). The author has had direct experience of this response and records the words of an elected member here: "I'd rather die than work with these people" referring to the range of partners assembled in the room for the formation of the first LSP in the local area. An evaluation of the work of the LSPs by the Communities and Local Government Department (HM Government, 2008), confirmed that problems with elected members seemed to focus on the idea that their mandate was somehow compromised in a multi-agency partnership (p.8). In addition, there were problems with leadership and inter-organisational power relationships (HM

Government, 2008. p.9). However, all was not negative. Some LSPs were very successful and still survive, notably Surrey Heath, Adur District Council, Haywards Heath and some have changed their names or amalgamated with other partnerships such as the Health and Wellbeing Boards (Local Government Association, 2019). Where partnerships work well, where relationships and trust are strong, multi-agency partnership is an effective and efficient means of tackling serious local issues (Roberts, 2016) and is recommended by the World Health Organisation (Sethi, et al, 2010) as a vital approach to tackling knife crime, and by the UK Government's Serious Violence strategy (HM Government, 2018).

Chapter 25

Partnership, Cure Violence and the VRU

The partnership model is an essential part of the plan to fight knife crime. It has been a success, and is still a success in many instances, (Roberts, 2016) but we must consider a new, redefined way of working in partnership if we are to effectively reduce knife crime in our towns and cities. Wider networks are needed, such as those cultivated by the PCSOs in British cities and towns. These are networks of relationships, contacts and interactions that elicit local information and intelligence. This was articulated perfectly by R:1, (13 July, 2019).

> "You got to know people who know people in the area, you know what I'm saying? You got to have a network in the city: a network where like I know the uncle, the cousin, the friend of a perp[etrator]."

The Cure Violence programme in the USA similarly uses a network of people from local communities to "interrupt" the pattern of violence R:2, (11 July 2019) argued

> "First of all the violence interrupters are from the communities themselves. They have often done time and are well known. They have the credibility among communities, are known by everyone but are supported by Cure Violence."

Being known to everyone describes the network that Perry (R:1) refers to above. Cure Violence, and especially the local CeaseFire programmes are both predicated upon the partnership work that enables a concerted, jointly focused effort to address community violence.

The Cure Violence programme in the USA, originally begun through Dr Gary Slutkin's work which is referred to earlier in this book, sets out a public health approach to the rise in community violence, especially gun crime (Roberts, 2019). The aim of the programme was to stop the spread of violence by treating it in a similar way to an epidemic: through tracing and containment. It was first named "CeaseFire" in Chicago, later becoming the Cure Violence programme. In 2008, the USA National Institute of Justice undertook an evaluation of the work achieved by the Chicago CeaseFire programme, recording dramatic falls in violent killings of between 41 and 70% (Skogan, Hartnett, Bump and Dubois, 2008). The approach is one of "community justice partnership" (p.1) with agencies working together to tackle the violence. Although this programme was largely aimed at gun crime, the lessons learned are applicable to the UK knife crime problems and have largely been mirrored by the Scottish Violence Reduction Unit, originally set up in Glasgow (Roberts, 2019). It is striking that the Violence Interrupters used by the CeaseFire programme are similar to the Navigators used by the SVRU in Glasgow. Violence Interrupters are recruited from the locality and have often been part of the very criminal behaviour they are employed to tackle, having done time in prison or been actively involved in community violence through growing up in the local area (Skogan, et.al. 2008). They work on the streets, often "mediating conflicts between gangs and intervening to stem the cycle of retaliatory violence that threatens to break out following a shooting" (p.4).

The Navigators of the Scottish VRU work on the front line in local emergency rooms or Accident and Emergency departments in the hospitals, trying to intervene in the cycle of violence by engaging with patients who have been affected by violence, including knife crime. They too try to interrupt the cycle of violence through their intervention, but the Violence Interrupters of the CeaseFire/Cure Violence programme often mediate gang conflicts in real time, which differentiates the approach markedly. Furthermore, the violence interrupters focus on individuals within the community who may be at risk of committing a violence act or homicide or who are at risk of committing revenge attacks following a homicide (Skogan, et al, 2008. p.vii). It is not a programme designed to target very large numbers of people and does not work through other agencies such as in the VRU in Scotland where Navigators are sited in hospitals. R: 1 (19 July 2019) is currently working on Staten Island New York as a Violence Interrupter within the Cure Violence programme mediating local conflicts. These individuals are paid by the programme, they are not volunteers as with the VRU's Navigators. CeaseFire's Outreach Workers engage with victims and communities as well as the Violence Interrupters, as part of CeaseFire's group of "change agents" (Skogan et al, 2008. p. 9) both helping to connect individuals with partner services for support. The Navigators in the VRU also undertake this work, linking people with partner services and support in the community. Notwithstanding this, the successes of both approaches are well documented (Roberts, 2019; Skogan et al, 2008) and the value of the notion of violence interruption and working in partnership to support those affected by violence, particularly knife crime, is established.

The most impressive element of Cure Violence is in the reduction in the numbers of homicides where it is in operation. Where funding was withdrawn in Chicago during 2015, it has been shown that homicides increased commensurately, reportedly by as much as 58% (Apolitical, 2020; Grimshaw and Ford, 2018), whilst during the times of full funding for Cure Violence, killings dropped by more than half. Similar programmes were undertaken in Boston, USA, where youth homicides fell from 44 to 10 during one year (Lydall, 2019) and during UK Prime Minister Boris Johnson's Mayoralty of London, a similar scheme named Shield was trialled in three London boroughs with similar results. It must be emphasised that when operational, the Cure Violence and VRU programmes have been supported and funded by government at local levels in both countries, yet when any such scheme is subject to political funding programmes, there are dangers. Funding was withdrawn for the Cure Violence/ CeaseFire schemes as a result of various political changes and Skogan et. al., (2008) point out that reliance on state funding for the programme caused "instability" (p.es8) in its operations. Skogan et.al. (2008) also point out that there are "downsides" to being part of a politically funded programme. Money that is subject to political decision-making will often mirror the cycle of elections in Britain, with funding targeted towards initiatives that are likely to attract votes. At the time of writing, the Scottish VRU and its partner agencies have not yet been subject to wholesale funding withdrawal as in the USA.

Whilst we must consider the comparison between the USA and the UK against the backdrop of very different cultures and different weapons, (guns and knives) the tactic of interrupting the cycle of violence at source is one that has been successfully adopted by both schemes. Stopping knife crime at source, within communities and among perpetrators and victims mirrors the approach in the USA: tackle the violence directly, using the people who are or have been involved in violence, sometimes as perpetrators, to help restore the perceived damage to community norms (Skogan, et al, 2008. p.9). For CeaseFire this was an essential element using what they called "culturally appropriate messengers" (Skogan et al, 2008. p.5) and this has been shown to be effective for the VRU too as shown in this book. As explained, using people who have credibility and lived experience to engage with those in communities who are engaged in the violence is very effective. R:1 (19 July, 2019) of Staten Island, New York, is just such an example. He comes from the local neighbourhood, knows the area, knows the youngsters involved and mediates conflict by scanning social media and other sources to detect emerging problems.

> "These guys, they know me in all the neighbourhoods. I'm known here. I don't want to go on like that, so I'm trying to do something for these guys." (R:1. 19 July, 2019)

R:2 (11 July 2019) commented on the use of those who have experience of the violence within the Cure Violence/Ceasefire programme, arguing

"They have the credibility among communities, are known by everyone but are supported by Cure Violence. The workers are trained and paid (30.000 dollars a year) and have their own jackets/ clothes with the Cure Violence id on it. They go in unarmed."

In terms of using people from the community to interrupt the violence, the approach within communities is common to both initiatives, whilst in Scotland, the Navigators work alongside statutory agencies and the hospitals as well as in the community.

The partnership approach in Cure Violence

Significantly, Cure Violence is founded upon the notion of working with partners to tackle community violence. The first line of the "Who We Are" page on their website talks about the value of working with partners to address problems of violence: "that community partners and strategic partnerships are the keys to success" (CVG.org, 2020). The summary continues to identify health professionals and agencies, the healthcare sector and communities to help with the programme. To date, they have been "under-utilised" in the fight against violence. Other community partners are listed on the website in a scrolling marquee across the page. These include the courts, youth charities, healthcare professionals, the Healing Justice partnership, the World Health Organisation among many others. Partnership working is an essential principle, as argued by R:2, the Director for Science and Policy at Cure Violence.

"the whole aim of Cure Violence is to create a connected network of people who know what to do to defuse a situation." (11 July 2019)

What R:2 is explaining is an approach we are already familiar with through the VRU in Scotland. Both the SVRU and Cure Violence have adopted the Public Health response to community violence, set out by Dr Gary Slutkin. They both acknowledge and promote the crucial need for partnership working as a founding principle. As explained previously in this book, community violence, including knife crime is a "wicked" or complex problem (Rittel and Webber, 1973). It is not feasible or reasonable in modern society to expect a single agency such as the police or local authority to address the many complexities of knife crime alone. Partnership is an essential response, not a luxury in this situation. This is highlighted in the UK Government's Serious Violence Strategy (HM Government, 2018). Multi-agency partnership working cannot remain unsupported, politically inconvenient or too difficult any longer. It is good sense to respond to complicated problems with a range of agencies and individuals who can address each tragic aspect of knife crime from policing to health, housing, education, youth support, social work, community leadership, faith groups and central government. Good quality, trusting partnerships can and do work to address societal problems (Roberts, 2016).

Even though there are clear social and cultural differences between the USA and the UK, and the weapons used in community violence are different, the means by which we have jointly approached the problem of youth and community violence through using the public health model have clearly shown benefits in reducing the incidents of violence. The correlation has been amply demonstrated and has been working in the USA and Scotland, later so in London and the rest of the nation. But it has to be reiterated that the British government has not yet achieved a coherent policy approach to tackling the problem of knife crime. There is a remedy, however.

Chapter 26

The case for policy transfer
to tackle knife crime

The notion of policy transfer represents the movement of political ideas and policies from one country or area to another (Jones and Newburn, 2007). Policy transfer is a term which is described variously in such terms as policy diffusion and policy convergence (Marsh & Sharman, 2009; Dolowitz and Marsh, 2000), but it should be remembered that these are not terms that denote the same thing. There are important differences: the first refers to an outward movement or distributive approach whilst the second draws policies together and can be coincidental. For our purposes, and for the sake of simplicity, we will use the phrase policy transfer in the context of this research, because the important emphasis here is in the suggested direct transfer of a policy from one government to another for the specific purpose of addressing knife crime.

In contemporary public policy, the practice of policy transfer has become an increasingly important feature (Dolowitz, Greenwold, and Marsh, 1999). It originates from the publications of Walker (1969); Gray (1973) inter alia, who focused on intra-state policy transfer in the USA (Alemna and Roberts, 2021. Forthcoming). The basic principle of using or adopting a successful policy from other countries or areas represents common sense in policy-making and public governance, particularly in this case. Where the problem of knife crime is concerned, we frankly need all the help we can get in Britain and if policy transfer is a viable option, then this should be examined. This book reviews the evidence for possible policy transfer from the Scottish knife crime policy to those various documents currently in place in Britain.

In noting the success of the Scottish approach to knife crime, which is documented in this book, it seems sensible, at the very least to first review the Scottish policy to see what lessons can be learned and whether the knife crime policy in place there can be transferred successfully to Britain. We will do this with particular reference to the larger conurbations where knife crime has become such an urgent problem. London has been a focus for attention in Britain and in Scotland, Glasgow has featured strongly in arguments relating to the efficacy of the Violence Reduction Unit. Although the Scottish VRU also focuses on knife crime in Scotland, it must be stated that this is just a part of a wider initiative to combat community violence in all its forms in the nation.

It is clear from the evidence set out here that Scotland uses a very different approach to that adopted by the British government in public sector governance. South of the border, the political landscape has hitherto been characterised by the adoption of New Public Management (Hood, 1991) which advocated a more performance-based, private sector model in public sector governance. 'Professionalising' the British public sector to bring it into line with private sector practice was the ethos of the Conservative Thatcher government in Britain during the 1980s and 90s. It was sustained in many respects by the following Labour Government of 1997 (Richards and Smith in Christensen and Laegrid, 2006. p.186) and has been continued by the Coalition and Conservative government since 2010 (Colak, 2019. p.157). Performance management and measurement became the guiding principle for public sector governance and the practice of running the public sector as a business in itself was the new norm. The British government fully adopted this approach in line with many other countries, including the USA (Massey and Johnston, 2015. p.447) where NPM originated (Osborne and Gaebler, 1992). These were not alone. Many other countries adopted NPM including New Zealand and Australia. As the origin of NPM was the USA, this makes NPM itself a prime example of policy transfer (Dolowitz and Marsh, 2000; Marsh and Sharman, 2009). In Britain, the Conservative governments of the 1980s and 1990s adopted the NPM principles of private sector practice being brought to the public sector (Colak, 2019. p.157). For our purposes, the private sector-dominated approach to the provision of public services has meant that in Britain, the driving force has been 'economy, efficiency and effectiveness' (Micheli, Mason, Kennerly and Wilcox, 2005). Some may argue that this has been at the expense of public sector service quality and the ethos of public services as a not for profit institution (Diefenbach, 2009; Chomsky, 1999; Micheli et al, 2005).

The Micheli et al paper (2005) referred to above looks at the issue of quality in the application of NPM. Where the drive has been for the three "e's", the reports analysed in the paper tell what the authors call a "different story" (p.1) where quality is often viewed as a luxury or unnecessary complication under NPM. The quality of public sector service delivery often lays in the qualitative element of the interaction between departments, partners and individuals (Roberts, 2016). Instead, quality in UK public service delivery appears to have been a casualty of NPM (Rhodes, 1998; Diefenbach, 2009). Micheli et al (2005) consider what they call the "productivity paradox", a term familiar to Information technology professionals, in which quality and productivity must be considered together for the purpose of efficiency. The productivity in good quality public services in which partnership and collaborative working can enable, rather than retard service delivery, has in many respects been sacrificed on the altar of NPM (Diefenbach, 2009) through the "commodification of services" (p.4). Here public services become units of production such as protecting looked-after children through the private sector companies who look to make a profit (Jones, 2015); converting the probation service into a half-private, half publicly-run enterprise (Teague, 2013; Teague, 2016) or academizing the schools (West and Bailey, 2013; Exley, 2017).

The interconnectedness of good quality, high-functioning partnership is discussed elsewhere in this book, but it cannot be overstated that much of the collaborative richness present in such services has been lost in the last three decades of NPM (Roberts, 2016; Diefenbach, 2009). Perhaps, to some extent, this may account for the fragmented nature of our approach to knife crime policy in England with an outdated policy document (HM Government, 2010 (b)), a Serious Violence Strategy which has no legal standing (HM Government, 2018) and a plethora of separate parliamentary library and committee reports.

However, in Scotland, the introduction in 2007 of the National Performance Framework (NPF) was the most significant change towards a different, more collaborative mode of governance for the public sector. The NPF represents the Scottish Government's own outcomes-based approach to public sector reform and performance management. It is argued here that the focus on outcomes rather than outputs as in NPM, supports public services and key contributors to work together in partnership. In other words, collaborative working became part of the Scottish government's official governance model for public services. Such collaborative approaches to tackling knife crime are advocated in the British Government's Serious Violence Strategy (HM Government. 2018, Ch.5):

> "Effective local partnerships and local multi-agency working are at the very heart of a successful approach to tackle serious violence issues......... only through a multiple strand approach will local partnerships be able to effectively identify, understand and tackle the serios violence challenges within their communities." (p. 70)

It should be emphasised here that the NPF served as a backdrop for policy-making in Scotland. The model supports organisations to align themselves around a common set of goals defined in terms of benefits to the Scottish people, rather than placing the emphasis upon quantitative performance-measured service delivery (Scottish Government, 2020). The Scottish approach to public sector reform encapsulates a move within public services away from top-down, service-led, reactive delivery, towards more personalised, preventative and collaborative way of working. It reflects more of a New Public Governance approach to public sector reform characterised by a plural or pluralist state: inter-organisational governance with an emphasis on services' processes and outcomes (Osborne, 2010).

Where in New Public Management a great deal of importance was attached to the measurement of outputs (both individual and organisational), New Public Governance pays more attention to how different organisations interact to achieve a higher level of desired results: the outcomes required by citizens and stakeholders. Moreover, in public governance, the ways in which decisions are reached – the processes by which different stakeholders interact – are also seen to have major importance in themselves, whatever the outputs or outcomes (Bovaird and Loffler, 2009). There is an important distinction in the approach that the Scottish and British governments have taken. Whereas in Britain, the move towards a private sector model of performance measurement, efficiency and effectiveness dominated the public sector, Scotland took a different path and embraced the notion of collaboration, partnership and network governance. Positive outcomes for the Scottish people were, and are, the end goal whereas in Britain, the focus has been upon outputs and performance measurement. This should be remembered when considering the different approaches to knife crime. In Britain the call was emphatically made within the Serious Violence Strategy (HM Government, 2018) for better partnership and collaborative working to combat knife crime. The current British policy approach reflects a late-coming to the idea of closer working with others. Instead, the British government have a piecemeal, un-co-ordinated policy platform for knife crime.

i) A review of the Scottish policy

The Scottish government present a single cohesive policy statement for knife crime which is readily available on their website (Scottish Govt. 2020). It is an accessible, relatively short and well-expressed policy document, detailing an entire partnership focused approach to the problem. The policy sets out a public health method for tackling knife crime, treating the violence as though it were similar to an epidemic (Roberts, 2019; Slutkin, Ransford and Decker in Maltz and Rice, (Eds) 2013. p.42) requiring containment and eradication. This approach is well documented both in Britain and the USA (SVRU, 2020) and has been followed by many others including the British Government, but in a fragmented manner. London Mayor, Sadiq Khan announced that the Scottish epidemiological approach was to be adopted when he set up a Violence Reduction Unit in London in 2018 (The Guardian, (c) 2018). However, it must be noted that according to the policy document set out by the Scottish Government, the VRU is part of a wide range of connected initiatives intended to tackle community violence and knife crime in a collaborative way. During the author's field research in Glasgow, respondents described this detailed, partnership approach, supporting the content of the policy document. The network consists of

1. The Violence Reduction Unit

2. The Navigator programme which sites volunteers in hospitals to approach victims of knife crime with a view to supporting them out of a violent lifestyle. Navigators approach people in the emergency department and continue to work with them after discharge.

3. Medics Against Violence which is intended to help educate secondary school children away from violence. This is achieved through NHS professionals speaking to children about the consequences of knife crime and violence

4. Mentors in Violence Prevention Programme which was developed by the VRU and promotes positive relationships via health and wellbeing. The programme is delivered through Education Scotland

5. No Knives Better Lives programme which works through local partnerships to engage with young people and raise awareness of the dangers of carrying a knife. This programme was explained to the author during the field research and will be discussed below.

6. Police Scotland Youth Volunteers. This police-led programme engages with young people to help them achieve leadership skills and confidence. Concentrating on the key age groups involved in knife crime and youth violence, the programme is targeted at youths ages 13-18. (Gov.Scot., 2020)

The foregoing represents a focused, youth-centred collection of initiatives to tackle violence which are well connected and visibly led by the Scottish Government. In addition, other agencies support these policy areas. For example, local authorities support the policy through interventions such as Operation Modulus, (Brunner and Watson, 2016) and Choiceworks (Glasgow City Council, 2020) for example. Operation Modulus is an initiative which was explored during the field research for this book in Glasgow. It is a highly successful, award-winning intervention targeted at a gang of youngsters in Gorbals area of Glasgow to tackle crime and violence. The above-named report identifies the success factors for Operation Modulus, and significantly, these include partnership-based leadership, sustained partnership working between agencies, co-producing the programme with young people and focusing the whole programme on the intended outcomes: to reduce the violence and tackle criminality. It must be noted, therefore, that the most significant success factor in this programme was the partnership approach. Similarly, Choiceworks is a related initiative on the part of the local authority which is focused on tackling anti-social behaviour and the causes of crime (Glasgow City Council, 2020). Choiceworks is aimed at those 16 and over and participants must have been involved in offending, live in Glasgow and not be in education, employment or training (NEET). What Operation Modulus and the Choiceworks initiative have achieved in Glasgow is that

> "...individuals see it as the chance to change the mindset and perception [of the police and local authorities] in the community.......working in partnership with police Scotland and other community based services allows us to provide an extensive support network where the client is at the centre." (R:27. 3 September, 2019)

No Knives: Better Lives (NKBL, 2020) is a major part of the approach in Scotland to tackle and reduce knife crime. Again, it works closely with the VRU as one of its key partners to address the many issues surrounding youth violence and knife crime. Supported by the Scottish Government and based at Youthlink Scotland (NKBL, 2020) it has collaborative working at its core, supporting partners in 11 local areas to implement No Knives Better Lives in each locality. Support from NKBL is available to all Scottish local authority areas now. The approach includes online training packages for their practitioners, peer education and training, educational toolkits for youth settings and schools, films, posters and a range of other resources to promote and spread the message (NKBL, 2020). Again, the partnership philosophy is visible in the close joint working with all other partners who are included in the Scottish policy.

The Campus Cops initiative, on the part of Police Scotland is part of this picture and has been described elsewhere in this book. It is, however, a crucial part of the partnership landscape in that schools and police are working together to improve relationships with the children, their parents and the community (R: 26. 3 September, 2019). Campus Cops are sited with the schools, developing long term relationships across education and communities whilst sustaining vital intelligence links in localities throughout Glasgow. Although sometimes challenging to begin with, where school heads are asked to work as part of a management move to tackle community violence, the Campus Cops programme is successful and seems to work well (R:20. 3 September, 2019; R:26. 4 September, 2019).

R:19 (3 September, 2019) explained the approach supported by Police Scotland, calling it a collaborative exercise, a coalition that stays in touch on a daily basis and meets regularly. The front page of the Annual Reporter for Glasgow Community Partnership (2017-18) has a headline quote from Dr Campbell Christie which reads "unless Scotland embraces a radical new, collaborative culture throughout our public services, both budgets and provision will buckle under the strain." It is the wholesale commitment to collaboration and partnership that characterises the ethos in Glasgow and which appears to have made the difference. Furthermore, 'One Glasgow' is an initiative that concentrates on young people aged 12-25 and is intended to bring about a positive system of support to reduce reoffending. It is a partnership-based referral system that links to social workers and is based on sharing information. The key feature of this initiative is that it is founded on what R: 19 called a "whole systems approach" which concentrates on three elements:

1. Early and Effective Intervention
2. Diversion from prosecution
3. Re-integration and transmission

It is based upon strong evidence that this integrated, whole systems methodology yields results and the evidence supports this. Overall Recorded crime for under 25s from 2012-2016 was reduced by 15.6%; there were 3,017 fewer crimes committed and this equated to £2.1 million of savings (Scottish Government, 2020). The point here is that collaboration and partnership yield quantifiable results.

With reference to the One Glasgow tripartite, whole-systems approach above: early intervention is strongly supported in the UK's Serious Violence Strategy (HM Government, 2018 p.57) and Diversion is obliquely mentioned in the recommendation to include involvement in sporting activities for offenders but support for re-integration and transmission from prison back into society has less of a focus. Evidence from the current research has shown a poor response to re-integration in England with R: 7 (31 July, 2019) reporting no integration activity in prison and no support for transmission.

SR "So you came out with nothing?"

R: 7 "I come out with a drugs habit man" (R: 7. 31 July, 2019)

The key lesson to take from the Scottish approach to impacting knife crime and community violence positively is that partnerships are on the whole well-structured, properly resourced and supported, multi-agency, vibrantly networked and strongly inclusive. These are all communicative, interrelated initiatives which are undertaken through the strong networks and partnerships existing in Glasgow and in other Scottish cities, but crucially, they keep the client at both front and centre of the focus. The emphasis on partnership working allows these initiatives to succeed.

Not so in Britain (Roberts, 2016). Partnership working, alongside other public sector initiatives, has suffered from the great extent of public sector funding cuts (Roberts, 2019). Officers are often not to be spared from front line policing to attend partnership meetings, in the police force and in local authorities. Opportunity costs cannot be covered when officers are absent from their duties, sometimes for up to half a day, to attend a multi-agency partnership meeting. Therefore, logic appears to point to the clear learning point here: that it is incumbent on the British government to learn from the Scottish approach of supporting and resourcing partnership and collaborative networking across communities. We know that this approach works because the British Home Office and London Mayor have both tried to emulate the Scottish model as a successful means to tackle knife crime. But it must be remembered that setting up a network of locally-based "VRUs" will not be enough on their own (HM Government, 2019 (d)). The Scottish Violence Reduction Unit in Glasgow was not set up simply to tackle knife crime alone. It is part of a co-ordinated, well-organised, partnered initiative to address violence in communities and this includes knife crime. The British Government announced £35 Million for 18 Police and Crime Commissioners to set up VRUs, based on the Scottish model in England (Gov.uk. 2020 (a)). The Scottish VRU as part of an established, collaborative environment, is set out in the Scottish Government's policy document shown above. It will not be sufficient to take a small fraction of the Scottish policy and hope that this will make the difference to knife crime without the infrastructure to support it in a similar way. Moreover, the initial £35 million supplied for setting up the VRUs had to be spent by March 2020, giving Police and Crime Commissioners only 6 months to establish them. It seems at best naive to imagine that a difference can be made in such a small amount of time. Scotland has not denuded its public services of funds in the same way and to the same extent that we have in England (Roberts, 2019; Institute for Fiscal Studies, 2015; Institute for Fiscal Studies, 2017; JRF, 2015 (b)) although the Scottish Government have levelled cuts against public services (The Scotsman, 21 May, 2018). Having said that, the field research for this book revealed that cuts to partnership working have not been as sustained or as deep in Scotland, though this may change.

ii) The British policy

The British approach to knife crime in terms of policy does not appear to be an updated (in the last five years) and cohesive document. The existing knife crime policy (HM Government, 2010 (b)) does not seem to have been recently revisited to take account of the rise in knife crime offences and murders since 2018. In other words, the current knife crime policy has not been reissued as a focused knife crime policy document in response to the rapidly changing circumstances of rising offences. Instead, various policy statements and strategies have been produced over the last five years, including the very significant Serious Violence Strategy (HM Government, 2018) which sets out a detailed response to knife crime. However, it is not a policy document. The various statements issued over the last five years do not seem to coalesce into a single policy statement or document. The following list demonstrates the fragmentation referred to above

1. Serious Violence Strategy (HM Government, 2018)

2. 2010-2015 knife, gun and gang crime policy (HM Government, 2010 (b))

3. The House of Lords 2019 Library Briefing Knife Crime Government Policy Debate (House of Lords, 2019) which reviews the various criminal justice responses brought in by the Government (p.1)

whilst acknowledging the feeling that not enough has been done to tackle the problem. It should also be noted that the document mentioned in (3) above reports a number of "initiatives" rather than a coherent policy (p.3). The Home Office also has an official blog which talks about their response to knife crime (Home Office, 2019 (b)). Over and above this, there appears to have been no update to the existing Government policy document on knife crime in recent years. That is not to say that what is in place does not have any relevance or application: on the contrary, the Knife, Gun and Gang crime policy (HM Government, 2010 (b)) sets out remedies for knife crime as expressed in the Brooke Kinsella report (sister of Ben Kinsella: a victim of knife crime).

- anti-knife crime presentations for school children

- more data sharing between police, schools and other agencies on local issues

- a best practice website for local organisations

- more work with young children to stop them from getting involved in knife crime

(HM Government, 2010 (b)).

These are good and sensible recommendations, but given that they were published before the current rise in knife crime in England, further attention should be given to this specific crime by the government due to the rising number of knife crime offences. Largely, the above-named policy concentrates on gangs and gun crime alongside that of knife crime. Therefore, it is now crucial that government policy is updated to take account of the many advances, both in the complexity of knife crime in England and the remedial actions needed through criminal justice, societal responses, probation, education, health amongst many.

The recommendation here, therefore, is to engage in a policy transfer exercise with Scotland. Engaging in such an exercise would give Britain the same focus as Scotland on knife crime. It is clear from the analysis undertaken in this book that we in England have sought to emulate Scotland's success. Moreover, the piecemeal approach taken by the English Government to set up individual Scottish-type VRUs across the country would be strengthened by the cohesive partnership support needed to make the VRUs a success if policy transfer takes place. The setting up of partnership and collaborative networks such as those in Scotland constitute the recommended response to knife crime in chapter 5 of the Serious Violence Strategy (HM Government, 2018). Yet adopting a small element of a successful policy approach is not sufficient to ensure policy transfer. To frame an analogy: it is rather like having half a haircut. Adopting pieces of a policy does not acknowledge the wholistic, integrated nature of the policy itself; the philosophy that underpins it; the values that hold the policy together; the notion of integration and collaborative working that make the policy a success.

A further issue arises here: that of culture and national context. It is certainly true to say that the two nations are very different, and the driving force of the policy against knife crime in Scotland is one of partnership, collaboration and integrated working. Here in England, the cuts to public services have seen deep fissures in public sector finances and widespread reductions in multi-agency collaborative working (Roberts, 2019; Diefenbach, 2009). It must be remembered, however, that knife crime has constituted a national emergency in Britain. Between England, Wales and Scotland, we share a common problem in which our young people are killing one another in record numbers. Where success has been demonstrated and proven in Scotland and elsewhere, we should at the very least consider the wisdom of this already established means of undertaking political process and decision making.

What is important here in recommending a joint approach such as that utilised in Scotland is that respondents in the research for this book supported this view without exception. It was victims, perpetrators, police, local authority personnel, charities, academics, community leaders and others who universally supported the view that no single remedy will suffice and that working together, in partnership, is the only way forward. In Chicago and New York where the Ceasefire/Cure Violence programme has made such a difference, a partnership philosophy underpins the whole approach (R:2. 11 July 2019; Skogan, 2006).

"... the whole aim of Cure Violence is to create a connected network of people who know what to do to defuse a situation. For example, a person is traumatised and about to commit violence. You need someone who is an Interrupter, [Violence Interrupter] who can then get in touch with the school/doctor/hospital/ or other agency who can then refer that person to the right mental health support service, the youth worker, the social worker who can then refer the family to wider support mechanisms." (R: 2. 11 July, 2019).

This bears striking similarities to the Navigator programme in the Scottish policy referred to previously. Partnership and collaborative working are essential remedies for knife crime. Individuals and groups who took part in the research for this book have a deep, shared understanding that a collaborative attack against youth violence on this scale would signify an effective joint response.

This links us back to the notion of Hermeneutic Phenomenology in which the lived experience of a phenomenon will lead individuals and groups to consider it in context and reflect upon it, identifying the connections between experiences. Respondents universally supported the notion that we must work together more effectively to stop the current surge in youth violence. Not a single one deviated or challenged this proposition. The key message for this book, therefore, is that we must work together more effectively. The ways that this can be achieved lay in policy transfer; using the Scottish model more holistically to address the problem; working together in partnership to include those who have been involved in knife crime and in responding to it, as in the lessons from New York and Chicago; legislating to restrict the availability of knives in England; utilising criminal justice remedies available to us in partnership with other agencies; co-ordinating the government response so that joint working can be re-established and redefined. These are common-sense remedies in an anomic society that longs to see the involvement of the state deployed to fight knife crime from the poverty and deprivation in communities to the legal redress in the courts.

Chapter 27

Conclusion

The evidence reviewed in this book, and that presented by those who kindly gave of their time and energy to answer the author's questions, paints a picture of inequality in Britain, manifested in its knife crime epidemic. If it were possible to draw other, more positive conclusions, they would be represented here. However, in looking at the context beyond the knife, at the reasons it is troubling us so much, we see solutions. These include restoring public funds to support services, working better together in partnership, including people from affected communities in our discourse and debate, and initiating a coherent policy for knife crime in Britain. Only then can we begin to visualise the removal of knives as weapons from the hands of young people. It is essential that the very losses suffered by children and young adults are reinstated. These are things which must be addressed at the highest level in Government. Failure to do this will allow knife crime to continue to evolve or will allow the recrudescence of this British pandemic in the form of the type of weapons-based violence we see that are rife in the United States. Already, new weapons are appearing in Britain, sourced from the dark web (RAND Europe, 2019) and this has been noted by Hampshire Constabulary, whose lead officer for this issue spoke to the author in 2020. Other weapons are beginning to appear in numbers and offenders are becoming more adept at using the dark web to obtain them (R: 29. 14 January 2020).

We have heard from those young people who have suffered disproportionately in a system that has become ever more divided over the years since the financial crash of 2008. We have reviewed the evidence presented by professionals and public servants who have watched the painstaking efforts of decades destroyed by policies of Austerity and deep public sector funding cuts. Britain is a divided nation, and that sense of division comes from its inequality. Data from the Equality Trust in 2018 shows that the richest one-fifth of households in the UK had an income of more than twelve times the amount earned by the poorest.

Figure 27.1 Household income by quintile groups

Household income by quintile groups

■ Original income　■ Gross income　Equivalised disposable income

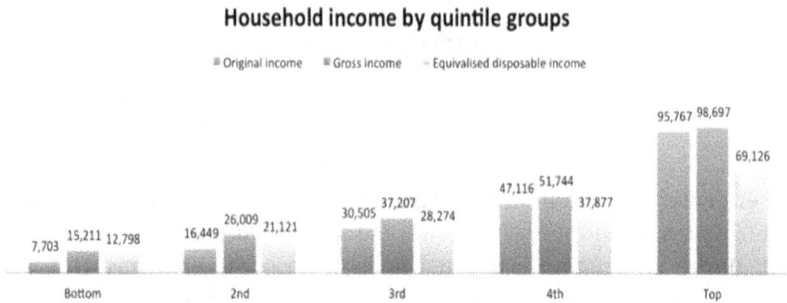

Source: The Equality Trust.co.uk

We are an increasingly unequal nation and the divisions such inequality causes only emphasise the ever-widening gap between the haves and the have-nots. We have heard from people whose lives are affected by all these factors throughout the evidence presented in this book. Everywhere we turn, inequality, poverty, deprivation, ruined life chances, racism, prejudice and self-interest face us and the pain of this realisation is heard through the voices of young people who have been wounded by this. We also hear of the difficulties and personal anguish our professionals face in trying to tackle and reduce the violence. There is no way to gild this particularly tragic story. Knife crime emerges from the context in which unequal conditions are prevail and they must be addressed as a matter of urgency. The problem of knife crime could be tackled through policy solutions and people working together, as we have seen. There are ways forward, as shown by the section above on framing solutions. If knife crime is not addressed, we will witness further violence and expressions of anger in ever-more sophisticated and evolving ways.

With regard to the findings set out at the beginning of this research, there are six major areas:

1. **Re-establish links with communities.**

2. **Deploy people who are part of the community to work with those involved**

3. **Redefine partnership working.**

4. **Reduce the punitive nature of intervention.**

5. **Offer young people real opportunities.**

6. **Use the lessons learned from others**

Each of these have been dealt with in detail in the foregoing sections, setting out how we can restore the relationships we to support better cohesion in our communities; how to use people who have experience of knife crime to help us to work with communities in partnership; how we can redefine our notions of partnership; how to demonstrate a less punitive approach to intervention; why it is so important to offer young people meaningful opportunities and how we can use the lessons learned from others whose policies have been shown to work well. It has been demonstrated that there really are ways forward for dealing with the knife crime problem in Britain. If the will is there, we can successfully address all the complex and difficult issues which have affected every level of our society so adversely. What is needed is the courage and dedication to grasp each nettle, and the hands that can take such action are located not just in government but in society too. We all have a role to play in this, and if we are willing and focused, it can be done. There really can be a path through the red sea of young blood that has already been spilled.

Acknowledgments

To the children and young people who spoke to me about their experiences, Police Scotland in Glasgow, the Campus Cops, young people, former offenders and all those who helped me so much. Thanks also to Barry Loveday, Ian Tapster, Paul Flenley, Mark Field and Tom Ellis at the University of Portsmouth, and to David Alemna for his support and insightful writing. In the USA, special thanks to Mike Perry of Staten Island, Professor Wesley Skogan, Charlie Ransford of CVG, and to Shelley and Mark for hosting me in Williamsburg.

Grateful thanks to my daughter Cate for her unstinting support and critical editing, my husband and my son for their love and kindness.

Bibliography

Agnew, R. (1992). Foundation for a General Strain Theory of Crime and Delinquency. *Criminology*. 30:1, 41-87.

Agnew, R. and Scheuerman, H. (2014). *Strain Theories*. Oxford Bibliographies. Available at https://www.oxfordbibliographies.com/view/document/obo-9780195396607/obo-9780195396607-0005.xml Accessed 12 December 2019.

Alston, P. (2018). United Nations. *Statement on Visit to the United Kingdom, by Professor Philip Alston, United Nations Special Rapporteur on extreme poverty and human rights*. Available at https://www.ohchr.org/Documents/Issues/Poverty/EOM_GB_16Nov2018.pdf Accessed 13 August 2019.

Apolitical, (2020). Available at https://apolitical.co/en/solution_article/cure-violence-cut-shootings-41-73-chicago-can-go-global Accessed 27 May 2020.

Audit Commission, (1993). Helping with Inquiries: tackling crime effectively. London. HMSO. Available at: http://archive.auditcommission.gov.uk/auditcommission/subwebs/publications/studies/studyPDF/1079.pdf Accessed 23 July 2019.

Barnard-Wills, D. and Wells, H., (2012). Surveillance, technology and the everyday. *Criminology and Criminal Justice*. 12:3, 227-237

BBC News, (13 December 2018). *London Violence: 'Concerns' over crime reduction plan* Accessed 23 May 2019. Available at: https://www.bbc.co.uk/news/uk-england-london-46538457.

BBC News, (8 March 2019). *Knife Crime: Are School Exclusions to Blame?* Available at https://www.bbc.co.uk/news/uk-47485867 Accessed 31 July 2019.

BBC News, (25 April 2019). *Food bank supplies help record numbers*. Available at https://www.bbc.co.uk/news/education-48037122 Accessed 27 August 2019.

BBC News, (4 June 2019). *South Yorkshire Police to cut half of PCSOs 'rebalance'*. Available at https://www.bbc.co.uk/news/uk-england-south-yorkshire-48515095 Accessed 12 August 2019.

BBC News, (18 July 2019). *Ten Charts on the Rise of Knife Crime in England and Wales*. Available at https://www.bbc.co.uk/news/uk-42749089 Accessed 29 August 2019.

Bloomberg, (2020). *Zoom Daily Users Surge to 300 Million Despite Privacy Woes*. Available at https://www.bloomberg.com/news/articles/2020-04-22/zoom-daily-users-surge-to-300-million-despite-privacy-woes Accessed 5 June 2020.

Bovaird, T. and Loffler, E. (2009). *Public Management and Governance. (Second edition)* Abingdon, Routledge.

Bradford, B. and Tiratelli, M. (2019). *Does Stop and Search Reduce Crime?* Centre for Crime and Justice Studies and the Hadley Trust. 4: 1-13. Available at https://www.crimeandjustice.org.uk/sites/crimeandjustice.org.uk/files/Does

%20stop%20and%20search%20reduce%20crime.pdf Accessed 21 September 2020.

British Medical Journal (BMJ). (23 May 2019). *UK's Austerity Experiment Has Forced Millions Into Poverty and Homelessness, says UN Rapporteur.* Available at https://www.bmj.com/content/365/bmj.l2321 Accessed 27 August 2019.

Brunner, R. and Watson, N. (2016). *Operation Modulus: putting Christie into practice in Gorbals.* What Works Scotland. Case Study. Available at https://whatworksscotland.ac.uk/publications/operation-modulus-putting-christie-into-practice-in-the-gorbals/ Accessed 5 March 2020.

Buck, D. (2018). *Local Government Spending on Public Health: Death by a Thousand Cuts.* [Blog post] The Kings Fund. https://www.kingsfund.org.uk/blog/2018/01/local-government-spending-publi c-health-cuts Accessed 16 July 2019.

Cambridge Dictionary, (2019). Available at https://dictionary.cambridge.org/dictionary/english/community Accessed 13 August 2019.

Centre for Social Justice, (2009). *Breakthrough Britain: Dying to Belong: An In-Depth Review of Street Gangs in Britain.* London: The Centre for Social Justice.

Chakelian, A. (2018). New Statesman. *Why are Councils Collapsing? Everything you need to know about the local government funding crisis.* Available at https://www.newstatesman.com/politics/uk/2018/09/somerset-northamptonshire-why-councils-collapsing Accessed 7 October 2019.

Child Poverty Action Group, (2019). *Child Poverty in London Facts.* Available at https://www.independent.co.uk/news/uk/crime/knife-crime-uk-children-nine-years-old-carrying-weapons-police-stabbings-a8613366.html Accessed 13 August 2019.

Children's Commissioner Report, (27 March 2019*). Excluded Teens are often the most vulnerable – and they're falling through the gap.* Available at https://www.childrenscommissioner.gov.uk/2019/03/27/excluded-teens-are-often-the-most-vulnerable-and-theyre-falling-through-the-gap/ Accessed 18 July 2019.

Children's Commissioner report, (February 2019). *The characteristics of gang-associated children and young people.* Technical Report. Available at https://www.childrenscommissioner.gov.uk/wp-content/uploads/2019/02/CCO-Characteristics-of-Gang-Associated-Children-and-Young-People1.1.pdf Accessed 22 July 2019.

Children's Society, (2019). *Our work to secure more funding for Children's Services.* Available at https://www.childrenssociety.org.uk/good-childhood-campaign/frequently-asked-questions?gclid=Cj0KCQjwyerpBRD9ARIsAH-ITn_E6oZIwrJaHqBFb4Dg9Z2MCjTaC9O9ax4yyXJ2FeFFXBukpyqLqX4aAhK3EALw_wcB Accessed 26 July 2019.

Chomsky, N. (1999). *Profit Over People: Neoliberalism and Global Order.* New York, Seven Stories Press.

Church Times, (2019). (7th June). *Hammond Rejects UN Poverty Report as 'Nonsense."* Available at https://www.churchtimes.co.uk/articles/2019/7-june/news/uk/hammond-rejects-un-poverty-report-as-nonsense Accessed 25 June 2020.

Clayton, J., Donovan, C and Merchant, J. (2015). The Emotions of Austerity: Care and Commitment in Public Service Delivery in the North East of England. *Emotion, Space and Society.* 14: 24-32.

Colak, C.D. (2019). *Why the New Public Management is Obsolete: An Analysis in the Context of the Post-New Public Management Trends.* Available at https://www.researchgate.net/publication/338363619_Why_the_New_Publi c_Management_is_Obsolete_An_Analysis_in_the_Context_of_the_Post-New_Public_Management Accessed 30 April 2020.

Comptroller and Auditor General, (2018). *Financial Sustainability of Local Authorities.* National Audit Office. Available at https://www.nao.org.uk/wp-content/uploads/2018/03/Financial-sustainabilty-of-local-authorites-2018.pdf Accessed 26 July 2019.

Creswell, J.W. (2007). *Qualitative Inquiry and Research Design: Choosing Among Five Approaches.* (Second Edition). Thousand Oaks, Sage.

(CVG) Cure Violence Group, (2020). CVG.org available at https://cvg.org/what-we-do/ accessed 14 January 2020.

Davis, R. (2008). *My gang, My Family.* The Guardian, August 9 2008. Available at https://www.theguardian.com/commentisfree/2008/aug/09/youthjustice.p arents Accessed on 22 July 2019.

Deas, I. and Doyle, J. (2013). Building community capacity under 'austerity urbanism': Stimulating, supporting and maintaining resident engagement in neighbourhood regeneration in Manchester. *Journal of Urban Regeneration and Renewal.* 6: 4, 365-380

Decker, S. and Pyrooz, D. (2012). Gangs, Terrorism and Radicalisation. *Journal of Strategic Security.* 4: 4. 151-166.

Demie, F. (2018). *Black Caribbean Achievement in Schools in England: Research Brief.* ResearchGate. Available at https://www.researchgate.net/publication/ 323175378_Black_Caribbean_Achievement_in_Schools_in_England_Resear ch_brief Accessed 22 July 2019.

Descartes, R. (1641). *Meditations on First Philosophy,* in *The Philosophical Writings of René Descartes,* translation by J. Cottingham, R. Stoothoff and D. Murdoch, Cambridge: Cambridge University Press, 1984, 2: 1-62.

Diefenbach, T. (2009). New Public Management in Public Sector Organisations: The Dark Sides of Managerialistic Enlightenment. *Public Administration.* 87: 4, 892-909.

Dolowitz, D., Greenwold, S. and Marsh, D. (1999). Parliamentary affairs. 52:4, 719-730

Dolowitz, D.P. and Marsh, D. (2000). Learning from Abroad: The Role of Policy Transferring: Contemporary Policy-Making. *Governance: An International Journal of Policy and Administration,* 13:1, 5–24.

Durkheim, E. (2013). *The Division of Labour in Society.* Basingstoke, Palgrave Macmillan.

Emerson, D. (2017). *Two Parliaments of Pain: The UK Public Finances 2010–2017.* London: Briefing Note, Institute for Fiscal Studies.

Exley, S. (2017). A Country on Its Way to Full Privatisation? Private Schools and School Choice in England. In Koinzer, Nikolai and Waldow (Eds) (2017). *Private Schools and School Choice in Compulsory Education. Global Change and National Challenge* Available at https://link.springer.com/book/10.1007/978-3-658-17104-9 Accessed 23 March 2020.

Fevre, R. (2016). *Individualism and Inequality*. Cheltenham, Edward Elgar.

Firth, D. (2005). for the Institute of Race Relations. *Schools Still Failing Black Children*. Available at www.irr.org.uk/news/schools-still-failing-black-children/ Accessed 22 July 2019.

Forrest, R. and Kearns, A. (2001) Social Cohesion, Social Capital and the Neighbourhood. *Urban Studies*. 38:12. 2125-2153

Frondigoun, L., Smith, R. and McLeod, I. (N.D.). *The Scottish Campus Officer, Past, Present and Future*. Available at http://www.sipr.ac.uk/Plugin/Publications/assets/files/Scottish_Campus_Officer.pdf Accessed 16 September 2020.

Fukuyama, F. (1996). *Trust: the Social Virtues and the Creation of Prosperity*. New York. Free Press.

Fussey, P. and Richards, A. (2008). Researching and Understanding Terrorism: A Role for Criminology? *Criminal Justice Matters* 73:1 37–39. https://doi.org/10.1080/09627250802277041.CrossRef Google Scholar Accessed 2 December 2019.

Geddes, M., Davies, J. and Fuller, C. (2007). Evaluating Local Strategic Partnerships: Theory and, Practice of Change. *Local Government Studies*. 33:1, 97-116.

Gill, K., Quilter-Pinner, H., Swift, D. (2017). Making the Difference: Breaking the link between school exclusion and social exclusion. Institute for Public Policy Research (IPPR). Available at https://issuu.com/ippr/docs/making-the-difference-report-october Accessed 5 November 2020

Giorgi,A., and Giorgi, B. (2003). *Phenomenology*. In J. A. Smith (Ed.), *Qualitative psychology: A practical guide to research methods* (25–50). Sage Publications, Inc

Glasgow City Council, (2020). Choiceworks. Available at https://www.glasgow.gov.uk/choiceworks Accessed 5 March 2020.

Glasgow Times, (5th June 2019). Glasgow Campus Cops 'integral' to Secondary School Life. Available at https://www.glasgowtimes.co.uk/news/17684221.glasgows-campus-cops-integral-secondary-school-life/ Accessed 16 September 2020.

Glenburg, A. (2019). 10 January. *Hearing hate speech primes your brain for hateful actions*. The Conversation. Available at https://theconversation.com/hearing-hate-speech-primes-your-brain-for-hateful-actions-107336 Accessed 29 August 2019.

Gov.Scot, (2010). Evaluation of Campus Police Officers in Scottish Schools. Available at https://www.webarchive.org.uk/wayback/archive/201704011 94142/http://www.gov.scot/Publications/2010/03/12111010/0

Gov.Scot, (2020). Crime Prevention. *Violence including knife crime*. Policy. Available at https://www.gov.scot/policies/crime-prevention-and-reduction/violence-knife-crime/ Accessed 23 March 2020

Gov.uk, (2020). (a) Education Maintenance Allowance (EMA) Available at https://www.gov.uk/education-maintenance-allowance-ema Accessed 15 February 2020

Gov.uk, (2020). (b) Funding for Violence Reduction Units Announced. Available at https://www.gov.uk/government/news/funding-for-violence-reduction-units-announced Accessed 4 May 2020.

Graham, L.J. (2018). Extending suspension powers for schools is harmful and ineffective. The Conversation. Available at https://theconversation.com/expanding-suspension-powers-for-schools-is-harmful-and-ineffective-106525 Accessed 1 August 2019.

Gray, V. (1973). Innovations in the States: A Diffusion Study. *American Political Science Review.* 67: (1) 1174- 119

Greig-Midlane, J. (2015). *Changing the Beat? The Impact of Austerity on the Neighbourhood Policing Workforce.* University of Cardiff. Available at http://orca.cf.ac.uk/65441/1/Changing%20the%20Beat%202014.pdf Accessed 9 June 2020.

Grimshaw, R. and Ford, M. (2018). *Young people, violence and knives – revisiting the evidence and policy discussions.* The Hadley Trust. Centre for Crime and Justice Studies

Hanifan, L. J. (1916). "The rural school community center", *Annals of the American Academy of Political and Social Science* 67: 130-138.

Hansard, (2019). Social Exclusion and Youth Violence. Available at https://hansard.parliament.uk/commons/2019-01-28/debates/0CC63C1E-1352-48E8-8699-E5AF40666B61/SchoolExclusionsAndYouthViolence Accessed 31 July 2019.

Hardoon, D., Fuentes-Nieva, R. and Ayele, S. (2016). Briefing paper for Oxfam. *An Economy for the 1%: How privilege and power in the economy drive extreme inequality and how this can be stopped.* Available at https://policy-practice.oxfam.org.uk/publications/an-economy-for-the-1-how-privilege-and-power-in-the-economy-drive-extreme-inequ-592643 Accessed 27 August 2019.

Hastings, A.N., Bailey, G., Bramley, M., Gannon, M. and Watkins, D. (2015). *The Cost of the Cuts: The Impact on Local Government and Poorer Communities.* Universities of Glasgow and Herriott-Watt for the Joseph Rowntree Foundation. Available at https://www.jrf.org.uk/sites/default/fles/jrf/migrated/fles/SummaryFinal.pdf Accessed 16 July 2019.

Hayes, G. (2017). Regimes of Austerity. *Social Movement studies.* 16:1, 21-35.

Heidegger, M. (2010). *Being and Time.* Translated by Joan Stamburgh. State University of New York Press.

Hemphill, S.A., Plenty, S.M., Herrenkohl, T.I., Toumbourou, J.W. and Catalano, R.F. (2013). *Children and Youth Services Review.* 36: 187-194. Elsevier.

Her Majesty's Inspectorate of Constabulary, (1997). Policing with intelligence. London: HMIC.

Her Majesty's Inspectorate of Constabulary, (2013). Policing in Austerity: Rising to the Challenge. London: HMIC. Available at www.justiceinspectorates.gov.uk/hmicfrs/media/policing-in-austerity-rising-to-the-challenge.pdf Accessed 19 August 2019.

Hesketh, R. F. (2017). *Radicalisation is not just a terrorist tactic: gangs do it every day.* Available at https://www.ljmu.ac.uk/about-us/news/blog/2017/11/21/radicalisation-street-gangs Accessed 25 July 2019.

Hesketh, R.F. and Robinson, G. (2019). Grafting: 'the boyz' just doing business? Deviant entrepreneurship in street gangs. *Safer Communities*. Available at https://www.researchgate.net/publication/334633203_Grafting_the_boyz_j ust_doing_business_Deviant_entrepreneurship_in_street_gangs. Accessed 16 September 2020.

Higgins, A. (2018). *The Future of Neighbourhood Policing*. The Police Foundation. Available at http://www.police-foundation.org.uk/2017/wp-content/uploads/2010/10/TPFJ6112-Neighbourhood-Policing-Report-WEB_2.pdf Accessed 19 August 2019.

Hirschfield, P.J. (2008). Preparing for Prison? The criminalisation of school discipline in the USA. *Theoretical Criminology*. Sage. 12: 79-101

HM Government, (1984). Police and Criminal Evidence Act. Available at https://www.legislation.gov.uk/ukpga/1984/60/contents Accessed 7 August 2019.

HM Government, (1994). Criminal Justice and Public Order Act. Available at https://www.legislation.gov.uk/ukpga/1994/33/contents Accessed 9 September 2020

HM Government, (1998). Crime and Disorder Act. Available at https://www.legislation.gov.uk/ukpga/1998/37/contents Accessed 15 July 2019.

HM Government, (2000). (a) Local Government Act. Available at https://www.legislation.gov.uk/ukpga/2000/22/contents Accessed 15 July 2019.

HM Government, (2000). (b) Terrorism Act. Section 44: Stop and Search. Available at http://www.legislation.gov.uk/ukpga/2000/11/pdfs/ukpga_2000 0011_en.pdf Accessed 7 August 2019.

HM Government, (2008). Department of Communities and Local Government. *Long Term Evaluation of Local Area Agreements and Local Strategic Partnerships Case Studies Issues Paper.* DCLG. Available at https://www.housinglin.org.uk/_assets/Resources/Housing/Support_materials/Ot her_reports_and_guidance/Long_Term_Evaluation_of_Local_Area_Agreem ents_and_Local_Strategic_Partnerships.pdf Accessed 15 July 2019.

HM Government, (2010). (a) *A Strong Britain in an Age of Uncertainty: The National Security Strategy.* London: HMSO. Available at http://www.cabinetoffice.gov.uk/sites/default/files/resources/national-security-strategy.pdf Accessed 23 July 2019.

HM Government, (2010). (b) Policy Paper: 2010 – 2015 government policy: *knife, gun and gang crime* Available at https://www.gov.uk/government/publications/2010-to-2015-government-policy-knife-gun-and-gang-crime/2010-to-2015-government-policy-knife-gun-and-gang-crime Accessed 11 March 2020.

HM Government, (2011). Police Reform and Social Responsibility Act. Available at http://www.legislation.gov.uk/ukpga/2011/13/contents/enacted Accessed 19 August 2019.

HM Government, (2012). House of Commons Home Affairs Committee. *Roots of Violent Radicalisation.* Nineteenth Report of Session 2010–12 Volume I. Available at https://publications.parliament.uk/pa/cm201012/cmselect/cmhaff/1446/1446.pdf Accessed 25 July 2019.

HM Government, (2018). *Serious Violence Strategy.* Available at https://www.gov.uk/government/publications/serious-violence-strategy Accessed 23 May, 2019.

HM Government, (2019). (a) House of Commons Home Affairs Committee. *Serious Youth Violence: Sixteenth Report of Session 2017-19.* Available at https://publications.parliament.uk/pa/cm201719/cmselect/cmhaff/1016/1 016.pdf Accessed 31 July 2019.

HM Government, House of Commons (2019). (b) *Impact of Social Media and Screen Use on Young People's Mental Health.* House of Commons Science and Technology Committee. London House of Commons. Available at https://publications.parliament.uk/pa/cm201719/cmselect/cmsctech/822/ 822.pdf Accessed 26 July 2019.

HM Government, (2019) (c). HCLG (House of Commons Committee for Housing Communities and Local Government). *Funding of Local Authority's Children's Services: Fourteenth Report of the Session* 2017-19. Available at https://publications.parliament.uk/pa/cm201719/cmselect/cmcomloc/163 8/1638.pdf Accessed 26 July 2019.

HM Government, (2019). (d) 12 August. *Funding for Violence Reduction Units Announced.* Available at https://www.gov.uk/government/news/funding-for-violence-reduction-units-announced Accessed 5 March 2020.

HM Government, (2019). (e) *The Timpson Review of School Exclusion.* Available at https://assets.publishing.service.gov.uk/government/uploads/ system/uploads/attachment_data/file/807862/Timpson_review.pdf Accessed 25 June 2020.

HM Government and Public Health England, (2019). *A whole-system multi-agency approach to serious violence prevention: A resource for local system leaders in England.* Available at https://assets.publishing.service.gov.uk/ government/uploads/system/uploads/attachment_data/file/862794/multi-agency_approach_to_serious_violence_prevention.pdf Accessed 16 June 2020.

Home Office, (2004). *Building Communities, Beating Crime: A Better Police Service for the 21st Century.* Available at https://assets.publishing.service. gov.uk/government/uploads/system/uploads/attachment_data/file/251058 /6360.pdf Accessed 19 August 2019.

Home Office, (2011). *Ending Gang and Youth Violence.* London: Home Office. Available at Home Office website at http://www.homeoffice.gov.uk/ publications/crime/ending-gang-violence Accessed 23 July 2019.

Home Office, (2019). (a) *Greater Powers for Police to use Stop and Search to Tackle Violent Crime.* Available at https://www.gov.uk/government/news/ greater-powers-for-police-to-use-stop-and-search-to-tackle-violent-crime Accessed 4 October 2019.

Home Office, (2019). (b) Blog: Home Office in the Media. *What is the Government doing to tackle violent crime?* Available at https:// homeofficemedia.blog.gov.uk/2019/06/18/what-is-the-government-doing-to-tackle-violent-crime-2/ Accessed 11 March 2020.

Hood, C. (1991). A Public Management for All Seasons? *Public Administration* 69: 3-19

House of Commons, Office of the Deputy Prime Minister, (2004). *Social Cohesion.* Sixth Report of the Session 2003-2004. Available at https://publications.parliament.uk/pa/cm200304/cmselect/cmodpm/45/45.pdf Accessed 13 August 2019.

House of Commons Library, (9 November 2018). *Knife Crime Statistics.* Available at https://researchbriefings.parliament.uk/ResearchBriefing/Summary/SN04304 Accessed 29 August 2019.

House of Commons Library, (20 December 2019). *Knife Crime Statistics.* Available at https://commonslibrary.parliament.uk/research-briefings/sn04304/Accessed 15 June 2020.

House of Lords Library Briefing (2019). Knife Crime Government Policy Debate. Available at https://lordslibrary.parliament.uk/research-briefings/lln-2019-0082/ Accessed 11 March 2020.

Housing Communities and Local Government Select Committee, (19 August 2019). *Local Services will continue to decline until government tackles £5 Billion funding gap.* Available at https://www.parliament.uk/business/committees/committees-a-z/commons-select/housing-communities-and-local-government-committee/news/local-govt-finance-report-published-17-19/ Accessed 7 October 2019.

Huffington Post, (19 May 2018). *Cressida Dick: Police Cuts Led To Rise In Violent Crime On London's Streets.* Available at https://www.huffingtonpost.co.uk/entry/cressida-dick-police-cuts_uk_5afff ae3e4b07309e0584c4d?guccounter =1&guce_referrer=aHR0cHM6Ly93d3cuZ29vZ2xlLmNvLnVrLw&guce_referr er_sig=AQAAALq4MSJmhh6b3JnGQkwh-8Vh75dyd4EbF7j1Tl8eYKBS_1QA2 Ej0qzeVzrzVGkvafcftV9w9CsvXhWhjVuj4OV8gZXPmCnnV587z6zCS3f4de2E YRdiJ2mjJfL0Ui2aR8Zn3Khp8HiUxW0hGqLcUvNeS41TWgKyxWPa_SPR8-Bai Accessed 25 June 2020.

Husserl, E. (2001). *Logical Investigations.* Abingdon, Routledge. (Abridged version).

ICT Police, (2020). National Intelligence Model. Available at https://ict.police.uk/national-standards/intel/ Accessed 8 April 2020.

Institute for Fiscal Studies, (2015). 1st October. *Recent Cuts to Public Spending.* Available at https://www.ifs.org.uk/tools_and_resources/fiscal_facts/cuts_to _public_spending Accessed 5 March 2020.

Institute for Fiscal Studies, (2017). *Two Parliaments of Pain: the UK public finances 2010 to 2017.* Available at https://www.ifs.org.uk/publications/9180 Accessed 26 July 2019.

Institute for Fiscal Studies, (2019). *Inequalities in the twenty first century: introducing the IFS Deaton Review.* Available at https://www.ifs. org.uk/inequality/chapter/briefing-note/ Accessed 27 August 2019.

Institute for Government Performance Tracker, (2019). *Neighbourhood Services.* Available at https://www.instituteforgovernment.org.uk/publication/perfo rmance-tracker-2019/neighbourhood-services?gclid=CjwKCAjw2uf2BRBpEi wA31VZjyVXwuBwsi3U08SdVQUbGFgrkYfdTlRZq3wSI18JtoQ-0AlQzcjomxo CC UYQAvD_BwE Accessed 5 June 2020.

Institute for Government, (2020). *Neighbourhood Services.* Available at https://www.instituteforgovernment.org.uk/publication/performance-tracker-2019/neighbourhood-services?gclid=CjwKCAjwltH3BRB6EiwAhj0IUHcYXE aaGJCKgeWCzoe2RnsI-ln5rOtGh1LmxRoe44viOJQ1N2lHwhoCMl8QAvD_B wE Accessed 25 June 2020.

Institute of Public Policy Research (IPPR), (2019). *Austerity: There is an alternative and the UK can afford to deliver it.* Available at https://www.ippr.org/blog/austerity-there-is-an-alternative-and-the-uk-can-afford-to-deliver-it Accessed 24 January 2020.

ITV Channel 4 News, (December 2017). *The Reality of Child Poverty in Britain.* Available at https://www.youtube.com/watch?v=FCMjfTkv9rY Accessed 22 July 2019

ITV News, (4 April, 2018). Available at https://www.itv.com/news/london/2018-04-04/charity-boss-gang-postcode-wars-have-spread-across-the-capital/ Accessed 18 July 2019.

James, A. (2013). Forward to the Past: reinventing intelligence-led policing in Britain. *Police Practice and Research: An International Journal.* 15 (1) 75-88.

James, A. (2016). *Understanding Police Intelligence Work.* Bristol. Policy Press.

James, W. (2018). *Essays in Radical Empiricism.* Outlook.

James, W., cited in Moran, D. (2000) *Introduction to Phenomenology.* Abingdon, Routledge.

Jones, R. (2015). The end game: The marketisation and privatisation of children's social work and child protection. *Critical Social Policy.* 35:4, 447–469.

Jones, T and Newburn, T., (2007). *Policy Transfer and Criminal Justice.* Maidenhead. Open University Press.

JRF (Joseph Rowntree Foundation), (2015). (a) *The most deprived areas have borne the brunt of local government budget cuts.* Available at https://www.jrf.org.uk/press/most-deprived-areas-have-borne-brunt-local-government-budget-cuts Accessed 24 January 2020.

JRF (Joseph Rowntree Foundation), (2015). (b) *The Cost of the Cuts: the impact on local government and poorer communities.* Available at https://www.jrf.org.uk/report/cost-cuts-impact-local-government-and-poorer-communities Accessed 5 March 2020.

JRF (Joseph Rowntree Foundation), (2018.) *Extreme Poverty and Human Rights: Response to UN Special Rapporteur.* Available at https://www.jrf.org.uk/report/extreme-poverty-and-human-rights-response-un-special-rapporteu r?gclid=CjwKCAjwqZPrBRBnEiwAmNJsNsi9BdzJt2ZZH0bnMg8cXIV8oEGCv WPmidQOg8ZyBsBe0vj6e9Lk-xoCBJcQAvD_BwE. Accessed 27 August 2019.

JRF (Joseph Rowntree Foundation), (2019). *Where Next for Universal Credit and Tackling Poverty?* Available at https://www.jrf.org.uk/report/where-next-universal-credit-and-tackling-poverty Accessed 27 August 2019.

Keeling, P. (2017). *No respect: Young BAME men, the police and stop and search.* London: Criminal Justice Alliance.

Kirchmaier, T. and Villa Llera, C. (2018). *Murders in London.* Centre for Economic Performance. Available at https://www.researchgate.net/publication/326318802_Murders_in_London Accessed 20 August 2019.

Laverty, S.M. (2003). Hermeneutic Phenomenology and Phenomenology: A Comparison of Historical and Methodological Considerations. *International Journal of Qualitative Methods.* 2:3 pp.21-35 Available at https://journals.

sagepub.com/doi/pdf/10.1177/160940690300200303 Accessed 27 November 2019.

Lazzarato, M. (2012). *The making of the Indebted man: An essay on the neoliberal condition.* Cambridge, MA: MIT press.

Leovy, J. (2015). *Ghettoside: Investigating a Homicide Epidemic.* London, the Bodley Head.

Local Government Association, (2014). *How Councils are Planning for Future Cuts.* London: LGA.

Local Government Association, (2019). *Health and Wellbeing Boards.* Available at https://www.local.gov.uk/our-support/our-improvement-offer/care-and-health-improvement/health-and-wellbeing-systems Accessed 15 July 2019.

LGiU (Local Government Information Unit), (2018). *The State of Local Government Finance Survey 2018.* LGiU. https://www.lgiu.org.uk/wp-content/uploads/2018/02/LGiU-MJ-State-of-Local-Government-Finance-Survey-2018-Full-Report.pdf Accessed 7 October 2019.

Lord, G. (2019). Profit, poverty and public care: austerity's charity work. *Journal of Organizational Ethnography. Vol. 8* (1) 68-81.

Lords Library, Parliament UK, (2020). *Local Authority Provision of Essential Services.* Available at https://lordslibrary.parliament.uk/research-briefings/lln-2019-0006/#:~:text=Local%20authorities%20in%20England%20have,roa d%20maintenance%3B%20and%20library%20services Accessed 21 June 2020.

Loveday, B. (2017). Still plodding along? The police response to the changing profile of crime in England and Wales. *International Journal of Police Science and Management.* 19:2, 101–109.

Loveday, B and Roberts, S., in Pycroft and Gough, (2019). A time of change: the expanding role of Police and Crime Commissioners in local criminal justice delivery. In Pycroft, A and Gough, D. (2019) *Multi Agency Working in Criminal Justice: Theory, Policy and Practice.* Second Edition. Bristol, Policy Press.

Loveday, B., and R. Smith. (2015). A critical evaluation of current and future roles of police community support officers and neighbourhood wardens within the Metropolitan Police Service and London boroughs: Utilising 'low-cost high-value' support services in a period of financial austerity. *International Journal of Police and Science Management* 17:2, 74–80. https://doi.org/10.1177/1461355715580913

LSOA, Lower Layer Super Output Area. Gov.uk. https://data.gov.uk/dataset/c481f2d3-91fc-4767-ae10-2efdf6d58996/lower-layer-super-output-areas-lsoas Accessed 3 September 2020.

Lydall, R. (2019). London Evening Standard 21 August. Shaun Bailey: *Ceasefire scheme trialled in US can halt knife deaths.* Available at https://www.standard.co.uk/news/london/shaun-bailey-ceasefire-scheme-trialled-in-us-can-halt-knife-deaths-a4218266.html Accessed 27 May 2020.

MacLean, R. (2020). *Understanding and Policing Gangs* Cumberland Lodge Report 2020. Available at https://www.cumberlandlodge.ac.uk/sites/default/files/Understanding%20and%20Policing%20Gangs%20Report%20%28screen%29.pdf Accessed 3 March 2020.

Marsh, D. and Sharman, J.C. (2009). Policy Diffusion and Policy Transfer. *Policy Studies.* 30:3. 269-288.

Mason, W. (2019). Knife Crime: *Folk devils and moral panics.* Available at https://www.crimeandjustice.org.uk/resources/knife-crime-folk-devils-and-moral-panics Accessed 14 October 2019.

Massey, A. and Johnston, K. (Eds). (2015). *The International Handbook of Public Administration and Governance.* Northampton, Edward Elgar.

Massey, J., Sherman, L.W. and Coupe, T. (2019). Forecasting Knife Homicide Risk from Prior Knife Assaults in 4835 Local Areas of London, 2016–2018. *Cambridge Journal of Evidence Based Policing.* 3: 1-20.

McCandless, R., Feist, A., Allen, J. and Morgan, N. (2016). *Do initiatives involving substantial increases in stop and search reduce crime? Assessing the impact of operation BLUNT2.* London, The Home Office. Available at https://assets.publishing.service.gov.uk/government/uploads/system/uplo ads/attachment_data/file/508661/stop-search-operation-blunt-2.pdf accessed 2 August 2019.

McNeill, A. and Wheller, L. (2019). Knife Crime Evidence Briefing. College of Policing. Available at https://whatworks.college.police.uk/Research/ Documents/Knife_Crime_Evidence_Briefing.pdf Accessed 15 July 2019.

McSmith, A. (2011). *No Such Thing as Society: a History of Britain in the 1980s.* London. Constable Robinson.

Merton, R. (1938). Social structure and anomie. *American Sociological Review,* 3: 672-682

Merton, R. (1968). *Social Theory and Social Structure.* New York. Free Press.

Micheli, P., Mason, S., Kennerley, M. and Wilcox, M. (2005). Public sector performance: efficiency or quality? *Measuring Business Excellence,* 9:2. Available at https://www.emerald.com/insight/content/doi/10.1108/mbe. 2005.26709bab.001/full/html Accessed 20 March 2020.

Moran, D. (2000). *Introduction to Phenomenology.* Abingdon, Routledge.

National Audit Office blog, (2019). *Local Government in 2019: A Pivotal Year.* Available at https://www.nao.org.uk/naoblog/local-government-in-2019/ Accessed 5 June 2020.

National Centre for Policing Excellence. (Centrex). (2005*). National Intelligence Model: Code of Practice* Available at http://library.college.police.uk/docs/ npia/NIM-Code-of-Practice.pdf Accessed 23 July 2019.

National Crime Agency, (2014). *National Strategic Assessment of Serious and Organised Crime* London: National Crime Agency. Available at http://www.nationalcrimeagency.gov.uk/publications/207-nca-strategic-assessment-of-serious-and-organised-crime/file Accessed 23 July 2019.

New Statesman, (28 November 2018). Dave Prentis article*: Universal Credit Has Been a Disaster for the Poor and Vulnerable: it must be halted.* Available at https://www.newstatesman.com/politics/uk/2018/11/universal-credit-has-been-disaster-poor-and-vulnerable-it-must-be-halted Accessed 27 August 2019.

NKBL (No Knives: Better Lives), (2020). Website available at https:// noknivesbetterlives.com/info/about-us/ Accessed 23 June 2020.

NSPCC, (2019). Website: Gangs and Young People. Available at https:// www.nspcc.org.uk/preventing-abuse/keeping-children-safe/staying-safe-away-from-home/gangs-young-people/ Accessed 22 July 2019.

OFHCR (Office of the High Commissioner on Human Rights) for the United Nations. Statement on Visit to the United Kingdom, by Professor Philip Alston, United Nations Special Rapporteur on extreme poverty and human rights. Available at https://www.ohchr.org/en/NewsEvents/Pages/Display News.aspx?NewsID=23881 Accessed 24 January 2020.

Ofsted, (March 2019). *Safeguarding Children and Young People in Education from Knife Crime: Lessons from London.* Available at https://assets. publishing.service.gov.uk/government/uploads/system/uploads/attachme nt_data/file/785055/Knife_crime_safeguarding_children_and_young_peopl e_110319.pdf Accessed 14 October 2019.

O'Neill, M. (2014). Ripe for the Chop or the Public Face of Policing? PCSOs and Neighbourhood Policing in Austerity. *Policing: A Journal of Policy and Practice,* 8:3, 265–273.

One Glasgow Reducing Reoffending. (2016). *Our Contribution to Supporting Positive Change for Glasgow.* March 2015- April 2016. One Glasgow.

Osborne, D and Gaebler, T, (1992). *Reinventing Government.* Reading, (Mass) Addison-Wesley.

Osborne, S.P. (2010), (Ed). *The New Public Governance? Emerging perspectives on the theory and practice of public governance.* Abingdon. Routledge

Oxfam (2013). *The true cost of Austerity and Inequality.* UK Case Study. Available at https://www-cdn.oxfam.org/s3fs-public/file_attachments/cs-true-cost-austerity-inequality-uk-120913-en_0.pdf Accessed 24 January 2020.

Panton, M. Walters, G. (2018). 'It's just a Trojan horse for gentrification': austerity and stadium-led regeneration. *International Journal of Sport Policy and Politics.* 10:1. 163-183.

Parker, J. (2015). Blog, *The Rise of Individualism.* Teamspirit UK. Available at https://www.teamspirit.uk.com/news-and-views/the-rise-of-individualism Accessed 29 August 2019.

Parliament TV. 2018. Home Affairs Select Committee, Minutes 9.45–9.47, 5 June 2018. https://parliamentlive.tv.Event/Index/f509cba6-db75-472d-885b-985cb5423aa1.

Parliament UK, (23 June 2011). *Service Provision, Funding, Commissioning and Payment by Results.* Available at https://publications.parliament.uk/pa/cm 201012/cmselect/cmeduc/744/74408.htm Accessed 2 March 2020.

Parliament UK, (3 October 2019). Research Briefings: *Knife Crime Statistics.* Available at https://researchbriefings.parliament.uk/ResearchBriefing/Su mmary/SN04304 Accessed 16 January 2020.

Parliament UK, (6 October 2020). Research Briefings: *Knife Crime Statistics.* Available at https://researchbriefings.parliament.uk/ResearchBriefing/Su mmary/SN04304 Accessed 14 October 2019.

Parliament UK House of Commons Library. *Knife Crime Statistics.* Available at https://commonslibrary.parliament.uk/research-briefings/sn04304/#:~:text =In%20the%20year%20ending%20March%202019%20there%20were%20259 %20homicides,the%20year%20ending%20March%202018 Accessed 26 June 2020.

Parmar, A. (2011). Stop and Search in London: Counter terrorist or counter-productive?. *Policing and Society.* 21: 4. Pp. 369-382. Available at https://

www.tandfonline.com/doi/pdf/10.1080/10439463.2011.617984 Accessed 9 August 2019

Picinali, F. (2014). Innocence and burdens of proof in English criminal law. *Law, Probability and Risk.* 13:(3-4), 243-257.

PPIW (Public Policy Institute for Wales), (2015). *Coping with the Cuts: Lessons from English Councils' Response to Budget Reductions.* Available at http://ppiw.org.uk/files/2015/12/Coping-with-the-Cuts-Final-Report-PDF.pdf Accessed 5 June 2020.

Putnam, R. (2000). *Bowling Alone.* New York. Simon and Schuster

Rae, A., Hamilton, R., Crisp, R., Powell, R. (2016). *Overcoming Deprivation and Disconnection in UK Cities.* Joseph Rowntree Foundation Available at https://www.jrf.org.uk/report/overcoming-deprivation-and-disconnection-uk-cities Accessed 25 July 2019.

Ramshaw, N. Charleton, D., and Dawson, P. (2018). for Mayor's Office for Policing and Crime (MOPAC) Youth Voice Survey 2018. Available at https://www.london.gov.uk/sites/default/files/youth_voice_survey_report_2018_final.pdf Accessed 14 October 2019.

RAND Europe (2019). *International Arms Trade on the Dark Web.* Available at https://www.rand.org/randeurope/research/projects/international-arms-trade-on-the-hidden-web.html Accessed 26 June 2020.

Ransford, C., and Slutkin, G. (2017). *The Handbook of Homicide.* Chichester, Wiley.

Reilly, D.A. (2019). *Finding the Truth with Criminal Investigation: Suspect, Subject, Defendant.* London. Rowman and Littlefield.

Rhamie, J. (2007). Eagles that Soar: *Eagles Who Soar: how Black learners find the path to success.* Stoke on Trent, Trentham Books.

Rhodes, R.A.W. (1998). Different Roads to Unfamiliar Places: UK Experience in Comparative Perspective. *Australian Journal of Public Administration.* 57:4, 19-31.

Richards, D. and Smith, M. (2006). in Christensen and Laegrid (Eds) *Autonomy and Regulation: Coping with Agencies in the Modern State.* Cheltenham, Edward Elgar.

Ricketts, A. (2016*). Cuts in public funding hit smallest charities hardest, says Lloyds Foundation research.* Third Sector, Available at https://www.thirdsector.co.uk/cuts-public-funding-hit-smallest-charities-hardest-says-lloyds-foundation-research/finance/article/1382975 Accessed 16 July 2019.

Rittel, H.W.J. and Webber, M.M. (1973). Dilemmas in a General Theory of Planning. *Policy Sciences.* 4: 2, 155-169. Available at https://link.springer.com/article/10.1007/BF01405730 Accessed 12 August 2019.

Roberts, S. (2016). *Just good Friends: Can Localism Succeed through Partnership?* ECPR. Available at https://ecpr.eu/Events/PaperDetails.aspx?PaperID=28250&EventID=98

Roberts, S. (2018). *Detecting Radicalisation in Communities: The Role of Multi-agency Partnership and the Power of Local Information.* http://rais.education/wp-content/uploads/2018/04/April003.pdf. Accessed 16 July 2019.

Roberts, S. (2019). The London Killings of 2018: the story behind the numbers and some proposed solutions. *Crime Prevention and Community Safety.* 21:2, 94-115. Available at http://link.springer.com/article/10.1057/s41300-019-00064-8.

Robinson, G., McLean, R. and Densley, J. (2019). Working County Lines: Child Criminal Exploitation and Illicit Drug Dealing in Glasgow and Merseyside. *International Journal of Offender Therapy and Comparative Criminology.* 63:5, 694-791.

Sanders-McDonagh, E. (2019). *Knife Crime: Why harsh prison sentences aren't the answer for young people who carry knives.* The Conversation. Available at https://theconversation.com/knife-crime-why-harsh-prison-sentences-arent-the-answer-for-young-people-who-carry-knives-113233 Accessed 2 August 2019.

Santos, H.C., Grossman, I., Varnum, M.E.W. (2017). Global Increases in Individualism. *Psychological Science,* 28:9, 1228-1239.

Scottish Government, (2020). *Crime Prevention: Violence including Knife Crime.* Policy document. Available at https://www.gov.scot/policies/crime-prevention-and-reduction/violence-knife-crime/ Accessed 5 March 2020.

Sergeant, J. (2016*). Are We Expelling Too Many Children from Australian Schools?* The Conversation, Available at https://theconversation.com/are-we-expelling-too-many-children-from-australian-schools-65162 Accessed 1 August 2019.

Sethi, D., Hughes, K., Bellis, M., Mitis, F., Macciopi, F. (Eds). (2010). European Report on Preventing Violence and Knife Crime among Young People. World Health Organisation. Available at https://apps.who.int/iris/bitstream/handle/10665/326377/9789289002028-eng.pdf?sequence=1&isAllowed=y Accessed 20 May 2020.

Shiner M. and Delsol R. (2015). *The Politics of the Powers.* In: Delsol R. and Shiner M. (eds) Stop and Search. Palgrave Macmillan, London.

Skogan, W. (1992). *Disorder and Decline: Crime and the Spiral of Decay in American Cities.* New York, The Free Press.

Skogan, W. G. (2007.) Police and Community in Chicago: A tale of three cities. *Policing: A Journal of Policy and Practice.* 1:2, 244–245.

Skogan, W.G., Hartnett, S.M., Bump, N. and Dubois, J. (2008). *Evaluation of Cease Fire –* Chicago. National Institute of Justice. Available at https://nij.ojp.gov/library/publications/evaluation-ceasefire-chicago Accessed 20 May 2020.

Sky News, (September 2018). *Map of London gangs territory.* Available at https://news.sky.com/story/london-map-shows-territories-of-dozens-of-gangs-11492542 Accessed 18 July 2019.

Slutkin, G. (2013). *Violence is a Contagious Disease.* Chicago, CureViolence. Available at https://pdfs.semanticscholar.org/15a3/194be46019051bba6be130029cd956f815f3.pdf Accessed 30 April 2020.

Slutkin, G., Ransford, C. and Decker, R.B. in Matlz and Rice (Eds) (2018). *Envisioning Criminology: Researchers on Research as a Process of Discovery.* Switzerland, Springer International.

Social Market Foundation, (2016). *Nick Clegg launches new SMF Commission on Inequality and Education.* Available at http://www.smf.co.uk/nick-clegg-launches-new-smf-commission-on-inequality-in-education/ Accessed 22 July 2019.

Social Metrics Commission, (2019). Measuring Poverty 2019. Available at https://socialmetricscommission.org.uk/wp-content/uploads/2019/07/SMC_measuring-poverty-201908_full-report.pdf Accessed 13 August 2019.

Somerville, P. (2009). *Understanding Community Policing.* University of Lincoln. Available at http://eprints.lincoln.ac.uk/2305/2/Rethinking_community_policing.pdf Accessed 16 August 2019.

Spalek, B. (2007). In Abbas, T. (Ed). *Islamic Political Radicalisation: A European Perspective.* Edinburgh. Edinburgh University Press.

Storrod, M.L. and Densley, J.A. (2017). 'Going viral' and 'Going country': the expressive and instrumental activities of street gangs on social media. *Journal of Youth Studies.* Routledge, Taylor and Francis. 20:6, 677-696. Available at https://www.tandfonline.com/doi/pdf/10.1080/13676261.2016.1260694?needAccess=true.

SVRU (Scottish Violence Reduction Unit) (2020) Available at http://www.svru.co.uk/ Accessed 5 November 2020

Taylor-Gooby, P. (2012). Root and Branch Restructuring to Achieve Major Cuts: The Social Policy Programme of the 2010 UK Coalition Government. *Social Policy and Administration.* 46: 1, 61-82.

Teague, M. (2013). Rehabilitation, punishment and profit: The dismantling of public-sector probation. *British Society of Criminology Newsletter.* No. 72. Available at https://derby.openrepository.com/bitstream/handle/10545/608589/bscn-72-2013-Teague.pdf?sequence=1&isAllowed=y Accessed 23 March 2020.

Teague, M. (2016). Probation, People and Profits: The Impact of Neoliberalism. *British Journal of Community Justice* Available at https://www.mmuperu.co.uk/bjcj/articles/probation-people-and-profits-the-impact-of-neoliberalism Accessed 23 March 2020.

TES (Times Educational Supplement) (30 September 2018). *Drugs gangs target excluded children.* Available at https://www.tes.com/news/drug-gangs-target-excluded-pupils Accessed 25 June 2020.

Teymoori, A., Bastian, B. and Jetten, J. (2017). Towards a Psychological Analysis of Anomie. *Political Psychology.* 38: 6, 1009-1023.

The Guardian, (12 October 2017). (a) *Pressure Grows to Make Universal Credit Helpline Free of Charge.* Available at https://www.theguardian.com/society/2017/oct/12/pressure-grows-to-make-universal-credit-helpline-free-of-charge Accessed 27 August 2019.

The Guardian, (18 October, 2017). (b) *Universal Credit Helpline Charges to be Scrapped.* Available at https://www.theguardian.com/society/2017/oct/18/universal-credit-helpline-charges-to-be-scrapped Accessed 27 August 2019.

The Guardian, (22 February 2018). (a) *I beg you to stop: plea from mother who lost two sons to knife crime.* Available at https://www.theguardian.com/uk-news/2018/feb/22/i-beg-you-stop-plea-mother-lost-two-sons-knife-crime-camden Accessed 6 January 2020.

The Guardian, (21 June 2018). (b) *The Radical Lessons of a Year Reporting Knife Crime*, Available at https://www.theguardian.com/membership/2018/jun/21/radical-lessons-knife-crime-beyond-the-blade Accessed 22 December 2019.

The Guardian, (19 September 2018). (c) *Sadiq Khan launches anti-violence plan based on Glasgow unit*. Available at https://www.theguardian.com/uk-news/2018/sep/19/sadiq-khan-london-mayor-launches-anti-violence-plan-based-on-glasgow-unit Accessed 5 March 2020.

The Guardian, (15 January 2019). (a) *London's gangs have changed, and it's driving a surge in pitiless violence.* Available at https://www.theguardian.com/commentisfree/2019/jan/10/london-gangs-changed-violence-waltham-forest-drugs Accessed 23 July 2019.

The Guardian, (4 June 2019). (d) *Stop and searches in London up fivefold under controversial powers.* Available at https://www.theguardian.com/law/2019/jun/04/stop-and-searches-in-london-soar-after-police-powers-widened Accessed 18 October 2019.

The Guardian, (17 October 2019). (e) *Knife Crime hits record high in England and Wales.* Available at https://www.theguardian.com/uk-news/2019/oct/17/knife-hits-new-record-high-in-england-and-wales Accessed 16 January 2020.

The Independent, (6th March 2017). *People Who Use Social Media a Lot are Isolated, Study Says.* Available at https://www.independent.co.uk/life-style/social-media-high-usage-more-isolated-lonely-people-study-university-pittsburgh-a7614226.html Accessed 26 July 2019.

The Independent, (11 June 2018) (a). *Drill rap gang jailed for planning machete revenge attack on rivals.* Available at https://www.independent.co.uk/news/uk/crime/drill-music-rap-gang-machete-attack-london-1011-ladbroke-grove-bedeau-a8393851.html Accessed 22 December 2019.

The Independent, (July 3 2018) (b). *Social Media Could Be Responsible for Rise in Lonely Children, Childline warns.* Available at https://www.independent.co.uk/life-style/lonely-children-uk-rise-childline-counselling-girls-teenagers-social-media-a8428166.html Accessed 26 July 2019.

The Independent, (1st November 2018) (c). *Children as young as 9 carrying knives amid "Wild West" violence in UK, police say.* Available at https://www.Independent.co.uk/news/uk/crime/knife-crime-uk-children-nine-years-old-carrying-weapons-police-stabbings-a8613366.html Accessed 13 August 2019.

The Independent, (22 May, 2019). (a) *UN tears into Tory led austerity as a "ideological project causing pain and misery" in devastating report on UK poverty crisis.* Available at https://www.independent.co.uk/news/uk/home-news/un-poverty-austerity-uk-universal-credit-report-philip-alston-a8924576.html Accessed 27 August, 2019.

The Independent, (18 July, 2019). (b) *Knife Crime Hits All Time High after more than 43,000 offences across England and Wales last year.* Available at https://www.independent.co.uk/news/uk/crime/knife-crime-uk-stabbings-record-london-police-violence-a9010201.html Accessed 12 August 2019.

The Scotsman (21st May 2018). *Councils in Scotland "suffer the brunt" of austerity cuts.* Available at https://www.scotsman.com/news/politics/councils-scotland-suffer-brunt-austerity-cuts-289608 Accessed 5 March 2020

The Telegraph, (25 April, 2019*). Knife crime rises to record levels but as few as a fifth of offenders are caught.* Available at https://www.telegraph.co.uk/news/2019/04/25/knife-crime-rises-record-levels-england-wales-homicides-hit/ Accessed 12 August 2019.

The Times, (3 March 2019). *The Scandal of Schools for Knife Crime.* Available at https://www.thetimes.co.uk/article/the-scandal-of-schools-for-knife-crime -8f90dt3f5 Accessed 31 July 2019.

Thibaut, F. (2018). The Mind Body Cartesian dualism and psychiatry. *Dialogues in Clinical Neuroscience.* US National Library of Medicine. Available at https://www.ncbi.nlm.nih.gov/pmc/articles/PMC6016047/ Accessed 3 December 2019.

Thompson, K. (2016). *Merton's Strain Theory of Deviance.* Available at https://revisesociology.com/2016/04/16/mertons-strain-theory-deviance/ accessed 23 January 2020.

Trussell Trust, (2018). *The Next Stage for Universal Credit: Moving onto the new benefit system and Foodbank use.* Available at https://www.trusselltrust.org/wp-content/uploads/sites/2/2018/10/The-next-stage-of-Universal-Credit-Report-Final.pdf Accessed 27 August 2019.

TrustforLondon.org, (2017). *27% of Londoners in poverty.* Available at https://www.trustforlondon.org.uk/news/27-londoners-poverty/ Accessed 13 August 2019

UNISON. (2018). (a) https://www.unison.org.uk/at-work/local-government/key-issues/cuts-to-local-servi ces/ Accessed 16 July 2019.

UNISON. (2018). (b) The Damage. https://www.unison.org.uk/content/uploads/2014/07/On-line-Catalogue2 25322.pdf Accessed 16 July 2019.

UNISON, (2019). *Youth Services at Breaking Point.* Available at https://www.unison.org.uk/content/uploads/2018/12/Youth-services-report.docx Accessed 16 July 2019.

Van Manen, M. (2016). *Researching Lived Experience: Human Science for an Action Sensitive Pedagogy.* Abingdon, Routledge.

Wacquant, L. (2009). *Punishing the Poor: The Neoliberal Government of Social Insecurity.* Duke University Press.

Walker, J.L. (1969.) The Diffusion of Innovation Among the American States. *The American Political Science Review.* 63:3, 880-899

Walton, R. and Falkner, S. (2019). *Rekindling British Policing: a 10-Point Plan for Revival.* Westminster, Policy Exchange. Available at https://policyexchange.org.uk/publication/rekindling-british-policing/ Accessed 16 August 2019.

Warren, S. J. and Wakefield, J.S. (2016). *Transcendental Phenomenology.* Available at https://www.sciencedirect.com/topics/psychology/transcendental-phenome nology. Accessed 14 January 2020.

West, A. and Bailey, E. (2013). The Development of the Academies Programme: 'Privatising' School-Based Education in England 1986–2013. *British Journal of Educational Studies.* 6:1, 137-159.

Whittaker, A.J., Cheston, L., Tyrell, T., Higgins, M.M., Felix-Baptiste, T. and Harvard, T. (2018) From Postcodes to Profits: How gangs have changed in Waltham Forest. London South Bank University. Available at https://openresearch.lsbu.ac.uk/item/86qq3

Williams, I. (2009). Offender health and social care: a review of the evidence on inter-agency collaboration. *Wiley Online*, 17: 6, 573-580. Available at https://onlinelibrary.wiley.com/doi/full/10.1111/j.1365-2524.2009.00857.x Accessed 15 July 2019.

Wood, R. (2010). Youth Deaths: *The Reality Behind the 'Knife Crime' Debate.* Institute of Race Relations, Briefing Paper No. 5 Available at http://www.irr.org.uk/app/uploads/2016/12/IRR_Briefing_No.5.pdf Accessed 22 December 2019.

YMCA. (2020). *Out of Service: a report examining local authority expenditure on youth services in England and Wales.* Available at http://files.localgov.co.uk/ymca.pdf Accessed 20 January 2020.

Youdell, D. and McGimpsey, I. (2014). Assembling, disassembling and reassembling 'youth services' in Austerity Britain. *Critical Studies in Education.* 56: 116-130. Available at https://www.tandfonline.com/doi/full/10.1080/17508487.2015.975734 Accessed 16 July 2019.

Zezulka, L.A. and Seigfried-Spellar, K. (2016). Differentiating Cyberbullies and Internet Trolls by Personality Characteristics and Self-Esteem. *Computer Graphics Technology Publications.* Available at https://docs.lib.purdue.edu/cgtpubs/1/ Accessed 3 March 2020.

Interviews

Respondent 1:   Mike Perry of the Staten Island True2Life Centre, CureViolence programme in New York. Mike is a "Violence Interrupter" (Interview 13 July 2019)

Respondent 2:   Director of Science and Policy at CureViolence in Chicago (Interview 11 July 2019)

Respondent 3:   Professor Wesley Skogan Professor Emeritus, Weinburg College of Arts and Sciences USA (Interview 30th May 2019)

Respondent 4:   Police Sgt. Police Scotland.

Respondent 5:   Offender, Milton Keynes prison, January 2019.

Respondent 6:   Group Interview, 30th July 2018

Respondent 7:   Young offender, 9 November 2018 & 31 July 2019

Respondent 8:   Youth worker, Croydon. 20 June 2018

Respondent 9:   Youth worker, London Borough of Hackney, 18 August, 2018

Respondent 10: Director of the Scottish Violence Reduction Unit, Glasgow, 12 November 2018

Respondent 11: Former Prison officer, London Belmarsh. 04 June 2018

Respondent 12: Former youth worker, central London. 19 July 2019

Respondent 13; Dr Brian Chappell, University of Portsmouth. Gangs and Gang Violence specialist. 24 July 2019

Respondent 14: Young former gang member, central London. 12 June 2018

Respondent 15: Charity worker and probation officer, 14 May 2018

Respondent 16: Police Community Support Officer, 22 April 2018

Respondent 17: Police Commander. Hampshire Constabulary, 21 August 2019

Respondent 18: Young former offender and victim of knife crime: Glasgow, 4 September 2019

Respondent 19: Chief Inspector. Police Scotland. 3 September 2019

Respondent 20: Police Sergeant. Police Scotland 4 September 2019

Respondent 21: Police Sergeant. Violence Reduction Unit. 4 September 2019

Respondent 22: Director Ben Kinsella Trust 21 August 2019

Respondent 23: Police Community Support Officer, May 2018

Respondent 24: Representative from Nuffield Southampton Theatres 6 February 2020

Respondent 25: VRU manager, Southampton. 6 February 2020

Respondent 26: Police Constable. Campus Cop. 3 September 2019

Respondent 27: Local Authority Intervention Officer. Glasgow 3 September 2019

Respondent 28: Former prison officer, London Pentonville. 4 June 2018

Respondent 29: Chief Inspector, Hampshire Constabulary 14 January 2020

Glossary of Terms

ACES	Adverse Childhood Experiences
ER	Emergency Room (USA)
GST	General Strain Theory
HCLG	Housing, Communities and Local Government
H1 and H2	Hypothesis one and hypothesis two
LSOAs	Lower Layer Super Output Areas. (Geographical data area for the purpose of the national Census)
MoJ	Ministry of Justice
Navigators	Volunteer force used in Accident and Emergency Departments by the Scottish VRU
PCSO	Police Community Support Officers
PTSD	Post Traumatic Stress Disorder
Violence Interrupters	First responders used by the Cure Violence programme in the USA to "interrupt" violence
VRU	Violence Reduction Unit
YMCA	Young Men's Christian Association

Index

G

gangs, 34, 40, 43, 46, 64, 65, 70, 75,
77, 78, 79, 80, 81, 83, 84, 85, 86,
96, 108, 116, 129, 143, 149, 152,
154
General Strain Theory, 10, 25, 26,
42, 43, 70, 139

H

Heidegger, 32, 33, 143
Hermeneutic Phenomenology, xv,
9, 10, 11, 25, 27, 32, 33, 39, 43,
71, 131, 147
Husserl, 25, 27, 31, 32, 33, 146

I

Institute for Public Policy
Research, 97

K

knife crime, xi, xii, xiii, xiv, xv, 1, 3,
4, 5, 7, 10, 11, 13, 16, 19, 20, 21,
22, 23, 25, 26, 27, 28, 30, 31, 32,
33, 34, 35, 36, 37, 39, 40, 41, 42,
43, 45, 46, 47, 48, 51, 52, 53, 54,
55, 56, 57, 58, 60, 65, 68, 75, 78,
79, 80, 81, 83, 89, 101, 103, 104,
105, 109, 110, 114, 115, 116, 117,
118, 119, 121, 123, 124, 125, 127,
128, 129, 130, 131, 142, 153, 157

L

lived experience, 8
Local Government Association,
55, 114, 148
Local Strategic Partnership, 113

M

Margaret Thatcher, 61
MOPAC, 85
multi-agency, 15

N

National Intelligence Model, 79,
146, 149
National Performance
Framework, 123
Navigators, 28
Neighbourhood Policing, 74, 143,
144, 150
New Public Governance, 123
No Knives: Better Lives, 126

O

Operation BLUNT2, 109

P

partnership working, 4, 11, 15, 16,
17, 19, 21, 34, 47, 59, 83, 118,
125, 127, 128, 134
PCSO, 47
phenomenology, 10, 11, 26, 27, 30,
31, 32, 33, 34, 42, 45, 155
Police and Criminal Evidence Act,
109, 144
Police Community Support
Officers, 22
Policing With Intelligence, 79
Post Traumatic Stress Disorder, 9
poverty, 10, 34, 35, 37, 38, 40, 43,
46, 54, 69, 70, 80, 86, 89, 90, 98,
101, 104, 131, 139, 147, 148, 150,
153, 154, 155
PRU, 40, 84, 85, 91, 94, 95, 96, 105
Pupil Referral Unit, 40, 84, 95

www.ingramcontent.com/pod-product-compliance
Lightning Source LLC
Chambersburg PA
CBHW050516280326
41932CB00014B/2338